Rogues of Wall Street

Rogues of Wall Street

How to Manage Risk in the Cognitive Era

Andrew B. Waxman

Published by John Wiley & Sons, Inc., Hoboken, New Jersey.
Published simultaneously in Canada.

For general information on our other products and services or for technical support, please contact our Customer Care Department within the United States at (800) 762-2974, outside the United States at (317) 572-3993 or fax (317) 572-4002.

Wiley publishes in a variety of print and electronic formats and by print-on-demand. Some material included with standard print versions of this book may not be included in e-books or in print-on-demand. If this book refers to media such as a CD or DVD that is not included in the version you purchased, you may download this material at http://booksupport.wiley.com. For more information about Wiley products, visit www.wiley.com.

Library of Congress Cataloging-in-Publication Data is available

ISBN 9781119380146 (Hardcover)
ISBN 9781119380177 (ePDF)
ISBN 9781119380153 (ePub)

Cover Design: Wiley
Cover Image: © Photo by.Ignacio Ayestaran/Getty Images

Printed in the United States of America
10 9 8 7 6 5 4 3 2 1

To my mother and father of blessed memory, Anthony and Lynda Waxman, who inspired in me a lifelong love of good writing and analytical thinking.

Contents

Introduction:
A Risky Business

The managing director for risk fixed him with skeptical blue eyes, "you are probably the most dangerous person at this Bank". I was incredulous. She wasn't talking to a swaggering trader. She was talking to her supposedly close colleague, the Head of the Global Policy Office at the Bank. The discussion for the last hour had been about the need to strengthen global compliance policies for Sales and Trading in the aftermath of the 2008 Financial Crisis. Surely, I thought, the danger must lie elsewhere.

Why do I open with this story? In many ways it's symptomatic of what was wrong at banks before and after the 2008 Financial Crisis. There were traders losing money hand over fist, in some cases, to the point of taking their banks over the edge during The Crisis, yet the MD perceived the greater threat as stemming from the Global Policy Office. Really? The pre-Crisis view was that traders should be left more or less alone by Risk and Compliance to work their magic. This did not work out so well in retrospect. After The Crisis a new belief took hold, almost as pervasive and erroneous as the "let traders be traders" view. The new belief was that rigorous enforcement of new policies and procedures would lead almost magically to prevention of wrongdoing. The MD, perfectly cognizant of this, was afraid that risk managers would retreat behind a bureaucrat's desk rather than engaging with day-to-day activity on the trading floor and that the effects would be just as bad as previously. Sadly, in her defense, to a significant extent it's my view that this is what has gone wrong after the crisis.

The evidence presented in this book suggests that both these factors have been at play in the years since the Financial Crisis. The strengthened regulatory and compliance regime imposed since the 2008 Financial Crisis this has not yet resulted in a corresponding reduction in operational risk events and failures.[1] Even a cursory reading of newspaper headlines in 2016 provides sufficient evidence of that point: Ponzi schemes, fictitious bank accounts, and cybersecurity failures are still common occurrences. The book's objective is, however, not to offer a critique of these rules and regulations or to argue that they are not needed.[2] The main objective of this book, rather, is to hold up a mirror to events caused by the Rogues of Wall Street—to analyze and understand them and then describe ways and techniques for identifying, mitigating, or preventing them in the future.

This past decade has been an exceedingly turbulent one for banks and the financial services industry. So many losses have been paid out to investors, regulators, and clients as either straightforward financial losses or penalties paid out for accepted wrongdoing. The trade date for many of these losses was the financial crisis of 2007–2008. Settlement date was often later—in some cases, as late as 2016—before the penalty was paid. Even in 2017, regulators are still announcing the settlement of cases with banks that go back to 2007 to 2008.[3]

I worked in operations and risk management at several large banks in the 2000's. As such, I participated in what are called "scenario planning workshops." The goal of these workshops was (and is) to estimate the size of potential losses in the worst of circumstances, black swan type events. I have to admit, however, that during these discussions, we hardly conceived of losses at the levels they have since reached. With multi-billion penalties incurred in some cases, it is now evident that banks failed to price these types of risks properly.

It is also apparent that financial crises hold special trepidation for banks and other financial institutions. This is largely because unknown operational risks[4] that, banks and other financial institutions hold on their books, are suddenly and ruthlessly exposed at such times. In 2008, bank losses suddenly ballooned from areas as disparate as credit default swaps, debt offerings, mortgage securities, money market funds, Ponzi schemes (Madoff), rogue trading, hedge fund positions and so on. Some institutions were pushed over the edge—Bear Stearns, Lehman Brothers for instance—while many others barely survived. This was no coincidence. Rogue trading positions, Ponzi schemes, even losses on mortgage securities, can be smoothed over, hidden by high profits, during the good times, but not during the bad times. Madoff's scheme, for instance, finally came to light in December 2008 after years of successful concealment. Driven by sudden cash needs, brought on by the Financial Crisis, multiple investors asked for their money at the same time. The demand for cash could not be met by Madoff's cash on hand and the harsh reality was suddenly exposed. This same dynamic played out across multiple venues, markets and positions. While it may have appeared then, that defenses were suddenly breached during the Financial Crisis, it was actually in the run up to the Crisis, that banks and other institutions were opened up, by and to, inside and outside threats.

This book suggests ways for banks and financial institutions to strengthen their defenses during the good times to better protect themselves during the storms that will inevitably hit from time to time. The acquisition of risk management capabilities linked to what I call the "Cognitive Era" are going to be required.

The Cognitive Era is referenced in the title of this book for two important reasons. First, the field of cognitive psychology pioneered by Daniel Kahneman and Amos Tversky, is in many ways a gift to modern risk managers. By leveraging some of this thinking (we will study some examples in the latter half of the book) risk management errors of the past can be avoided. Second, the era of "cognitive computing", that has been recently heralded by IBM and other proponents of Artificial Intelligence, presents new opportunities for risk managers.

Partly due to the availability of ever-increasing computing hardware and network power and also due to the availability of new AI (artificial intelligence) technologies, corporations now have cognitive digital platforms at their disposal to improve their ability to manage a wide range of tasks. These platforms encompass machine learning, reasoning, natural language processing, speech and vision, human-computer interaction, dialog and narrative generation, and more—systems that learn at scale, reason with purpose, and interact with humans naturally. We explore some specific applications in the field of surveillance and regulatory management that can support the ability of banks to prevent and mitigate operational risks more effectively in the future. Some of these techniques are already being explored and implemented in the field.

The first part of this book, Chapters 2 through 14, takes the reader through a "Rogue Gallery of Wall Street"—the characters and events behind the losses and failures at storied investment houses and securities firms in the past several years. We look at some of the factors behind the events, the causes, and some of the things that can be done to prevent their reoccurrence in the future.

The Rogue Trader, naturally enough, is the first character we come across in this Rogue Gallery. Typical of this archetype was the trading incident at UBS that occurred in late 2011 that resulted in a loss of over $2 billion for that bank. This incident was similar in many respects to the Rogue Trader incident at Societe Generale[5] only four years earlier that resulted in a loss of around $7 million. We will look at these characters and incidents in more detail in Chapter 2.

Rogue Traders, however, are not the only type of bad actor that investment banks have had to deal with in the past few years. The Genius Trader is the second character we meet, and, of course, is not always bad to know. As the name suggests, this character is very smart, perhaps too smart, and his colleagues and bosses give him more latitude to trade than other traders. The trades he executes and the positions he accumulates are very complex and not necessarily understood by his bosses or by the risk managers whose job it is to protect the bank from taking on too much risk. The losses that can result from these trading decisions and miscalculations can be very, very large, leading in some cases to the fall of a major financial institution.[6] We will look at the many lessons for risk management from this and other episodes in Chapter 3.

Insider trading has also been front and center in the past few years. Many of those convicted of insider trading have been traders at hedge funds. One of the consequences of banking regulations has been the multiplying of hedge funds established by traders dissatisfied by the resulting conditions at the large banks. The spate of insider trading charges at hedge funds, some of which may lack sufficiently strong and independent compliance oversight and surveillance functions, has perhaps been the logical consequence of that. The issues here and potential remedies are looked at in Chapter 4.

Banks also need to be aware that there may be price manipulators in their ranks. Traders at several banks were charged in 2012 with the crime of manipulating LIBOR rates, rates that are set by a group of specifically appointed banks. The foreign exchange rate manipulation debacle followed soon after that.[7] Wide-ranging investigations following both these scandals resulted in dismissals and even criminal charges levelled at several major banks. One may wonder justifiably why all the compliance and pricing infrastructure and policies and procedures that banks have put in place failed to identify these issues. We will look at these issues in more detail in Chapter 5.

Penalties imposed by regulators following mortgage-related litigation has been a significant drain on banks since the 2008 Financial Crisis. We identify the key risk indicators and lessons learned from these events in Chapter 6.

Meanwhile, threats inside banks and hedge funds posed by Rogue Traders and others are matched by threats posed by those from outside. Wall Street also needs to do a better job of protecting itself and society from these external threats: money launderers (drug gangs, terrorists, etc.), Ponzi schemers, cyberterrorists, social media, rogue technology, spreadsheets, and Acts of God. We will look at each of these risks and episodes in some detail and draw out what can be done going forward in respect of each one in Chapters 7 to 14.

Where the first part of this book catalogs some of the major risk incidents that have taken place in the last few years, the second part of the book, starting with Chapter 16, looks at the overarching tools that financial institutions have to work with to create an environment that can prevent and mitigate catastrophic events in the future.

The tools that banks have at their disposal to address these risks are first and foremost their employees. Whether or not employees are successfully enlisted in the battle is very much dependent on the culture that they collectively create. Chapter 17 describes a risk management culture that emphasizes the role of each employee and imbues in each a sense of mutual responsibility to the bank and to one another. Is there a sense of right and wrong that is as much a part of the bank as the financial language they speak? We will discuss the 360-degree risk culture at some length and look at examples and tools for making that happen.

In Chapter 18, will then proceed to discuss the importance of a common understanding and language to discuss and remediate the key types of risks facing banks today. What we are talking about when we talk about risk is something that each employee needs to understand from the top to the bottom. If one employee thinks of risk as one thing and his colleague thinks of it as another, then they will look past one another and fail to come together.

Chapters 19 and 20 discuss the classic paradigm of operational risk management—summed up by the words of the historian, Geoffrey Elton: "The future is dark, the present burdensome; only the past, dead and finished, bears contemplation."[8] Risk management has always placed great emphasis on studying the past. If one can determine the risk events and losses in the past, one can learn how much capital to set aside for future losses. If one can understand how much market losses there were in the prior period, one can identify the scope of potential losses in the future. While this approach may have been adequate in the past and does provide an effective measurement baseline, it is not sufficient for the future and so in later chapters we turn to explore newer, more modern approaches and techniques. It is not just financial loss that is at stake but the loss of reputation with clients and the broader community, as recent scandals have shown. A more ambitious goal set by the most innovative risk managers today is to understand the past, not just to measure it but also to prevent it from recurring in the future.

In Chapter 20, we turn to new tools of risk management that involve advanced cognitive understanding of human behaviors and motivations. The use of psychological insight and data analytics are tools that can create incentives and programs to prevent risky behaviors and drive employees toward improved outcomes in the field.

It is no exaggeration to say that proper and appropriate trade surveillance could have helped to avert or reduce the impact of many of the events that banks have been paying for in the past few years. In Chapter 21, we explore new cognitive AI tools that can complement the current trade surveillance activities to identify risky behaviors before they result in losses and reputational damage.

Finally, we discuss external factors, in particular, the role of external stakeholders, from regulators to society at large. The level of interdependency between institutions was shown for all to see in 2008 and needs to be studied to understand how a reoccurrence of those types of events can be prevented. This may be critical in helping our banks and society to avoid a repeat of the 2008 Financial Crisis in the near future.

Notes

1. It was reported in 2014 that Citigroup Inc. would put nearly 30,000 employees to work on regulatory and compliance issues by the end of 2014. That pushed compliance staffing levels up 33 percent since the end of 2011. Sital S. Patel, "Citi Will Have Almost 30,000 Employees in Compliance by Year-End," *Market Watch* (July 14, 2014), http://blogs.marketwatch.com/thetell/2014/07/14/citi-will-have-almost-30000-employees-in-compliance-by-year-end. Similar reports were filed for JPMC. Lauren Tara LaCapra and David Henry, "JPMorgan to Spend $4 Billion on Compliance and Risk Controls: WSJ," Reuters (September 12, 2013), http://www.reuters.com/article/us-usa-jpmorgan-risk-idUSBRE98C00720130913.

2. A key scandal was unearthed in 2016 involving Wells Fargo and retail bank customers. This seems to be something new. A Ponzi scheme was also uncovered at Platinum Partners. This was something old. http://www.nydailynews.com/new-york/nyc-crime/platinum-partners-hedge-fund-bigs-face-charges-1b-fraud-case-article-1.2916343.

3. US Department of Justice, "Deutsche Bank Agrees to pay $7.2 Billion for Misleading Investors in Its Sale of Residential Mortgage-Backed Securities. Deutsche Bank's Conduct Contributed to the 2008 Financial Crisis" (January 17, 2017), https://www.justice.gov/opa/pr/deutsche-bank-agrees-pay-72-billion-misleading-investors-its-sale-residential-mortgage-backed.

4. Operational risk is the risk that deficiencies in information systems or internal processes, human errors, management failures, or disruptions from external events will result in the reduction, deterioration, or breakdown of services provided by an FMI. http://www.bis.org/cpmi/publ/d00b.htm?&selection=48&scope=CPMI&c=a&base=term.

5. Jerome Kerviel, a French trader, was convicted in the 2008 Societe Generale trading loss for breach of trust, forgery, and unauthorized use of the bank's computers, resulting in losses valued at €4.9 billion. http://www.businessinsider.com/how-jerome-kerviel-lost-72-billion-2016-5.

6. Roger Lowenstein, *When Genius Failed: The Rise and Fall of Long-Term Capital Management* (New York: Random House, 2000). Lowenstein chronicles the rise and fall of the illustrious hedge fund Long-Term Capital Management.

7. LIBOR is a benchmark rate that some of the world's leading banks charge each other for short-term loans. It stands for London Interbank Offered Rate and facilitates the calculation of interest rates on various loans throughout the world. LIBOR is based on five currencies: US dollar (USD), euro (EUR), pound sterling (GBP), Japanese yen (JPY), and Swiss franc (CHF), and provides seven different maturities of each one: overnight, one week, and 1, 2, 3, 6, and 12 months.

8. G. Elton, *The Practice of History* (Waukegen, IL: Fontana Press, 1967).

Acknowledgments

I could not have written this book without the many colleagues over the years from whom I have learned so much. There are too many to name, but you know who you are. Thank you!

I would also like to acknowledge the following who have helped me to bring this book to fruition: Dickie Steele, my fellow Bowdonian in New York who provided insights and ideas right up to the final deadline; Josh Getzler, who provided the initial encouragement in my writing endeavors; Steven Stansel at IBM Press who helped navigate the publishing pathways at IBM, and Bill Falloon and rest of the team at Wiley who provided such brilliant support throughout this process. Lastly, to my family—you're simply the best!

About the Author

Andrew Waxman is an associate partner in IBM's Financial Services Risk and Compliance consulting practice with over 20 years of experience, in the United States and the United Kingdom, helping financial services organizations manage complex business issues.

Andrew has written on risk and banking issues in journals such as *American Banker* and *Wall Street and Technology* for many years.

Andrew lives in New York, where he shares his home with his wife and two daughters.

CHAPTER 1

The Historical Context

Wall Street has changed immeasurably in the past several decades. Key changes that have occurred include computerization of trading, the growth of universal banks (and hedge funds), and the development of financial engineering. Each of these changes enabled major revolutions to take place in our larger society. Banks are not what they used to be, but while they were agents in enabling change in society—changes that brought major benefits—with these benefits also came major costs.

First, computerization of trading has helped to facilitate the growth of a shareholder society. The casual, retail investor now has access to trading tools that provide access to very liquid and fast-moving markets with the ability to execute shorts, options, swaps, foreign exchange (FX), and other complex transactions from their PC or smart phone. The cost of participating in such trading activities has declined dramatically and, as a result, millions more people[1] own shares today than in the past. This has been in large part due to the creation of new trading and computer technologies and resulting cost reduction. Such gains are not achieved without risk, however. Some of the operational risk incidents we will review in the coming chapters stem from the technical challenges that are posed by such technological advances.

Second, the growth of universal banks[2] with massive capital resources and services aimed at every customer segment has helped achieve major efficiencies in the promotion of new capital structures and investment vehicles. The availability of credit to greater numbers of people and the provision of new types of financial innovation to every type of corporate entity has enabled the creation and expansion of new productive capacity in the United States. These advantages were particularly clear during the expansion years of the 1990s and early 2000s. However, these benefits also brought problems in their wake.

The sheer size of these universal banks and the stitching together of different legacy systems and bank cultures has created patchworks of manual process and controls that became too complex to manage. The risk of great and complex failures inherent in such unwieldy structures has, in the eyes of many analysts, grown, rather than retreated since the Financial Crisis of 2008. Most recently, Neel Kashkari, chief of the Federal Reserve Bank of Minneapolis, has argued for further controls to be put in place against banks that are so called "too big to fail."[3]

To his point, managing multiple businesses and multiple country branches brings a level of complexity that makes it much more difficult to monitor activities across an entire organization. Additionally, privacy laws that have multiplied in different countries have further exacerbated this issue. This can and has led to failures to assert centralized controls and unified lines of defense against suspicious trading activity and the like.[4]

Third, the growth of financial engineering took place in the context of relatively light regulation and planning. Credit default swaps, for example, started as a relatively obscure product in an obscure trading group within investment banks. While investment banks and broker/dealers are required to oversee new product development in a careful way, new products have a habit of getting through with relatively little scrutiny and planning. This lack of planning is, in part, a reasonable response to the nature of the trading market. Many products are thought up in the twinkle of a trader's eye and many of them fail to take hold. In the case of credit default swaps,[5] however, within a very short time frame, billions of them were being written to cover bondholders and non–bondholders. Expansion in areas like this brought much greater profits to the banks, at least for a time. It also brought much greater complexity to the business. Obscure products like credit default swaps can thus grow from a relative backwater status to a major profit center in a short space of time in a way that is hard to predict or plan for. The ability to manage the resulting complexity, however, does not tend to keep up. The rash of scandals, penalties, and significant operational losses in the case of mortgage-securitized products are one indicator of that.

The rapid change at investment banks as a result of these particular areas of innovation has made it hard for regulators to keep up in their ability to understand and monitor these changes. Yet the role of regulators has never been more important. In some ways, the battle over regulation that took place in the years after the 2008 Financial Crisis, and in particular, the battle to introduce the Dodd-Frank legislation was similar to that played out in the original battles fought by Washington and the SEC to establish US securities laws and the SEC in the 1930s. This will be discussed further in Chapter 22.

The battle fought by the regulators since 2008 has also been to arm themselves for battle more effectively, by adding to their ranks people with the expertise and experience to be able to identify, monitor, and manage the risks as they unfold at their charges' houses of operations. Unfortunately, it may always be the case that regulators, like the French generals of the 1930s who built the Maginot Line of Defense, are doomed to be forever fighting the previous war.

The example that perhaps best illustrates this is the case of Wells Fargo that hit the headlines in 2016.[6] This was different from what had gone before in three important respects. First, relative to the mortgage and other scandals, which led to billions of dollars in lost wealth, the churning of unauthorized bank and other accounts involved sums that were relatively small. Second, instead of a few relatively high level traders being involved, as in, for example, the mortgage, FX and LIBOR scandals, this scandal involved thousands of fairly low level employees. Third, those involved in the scandal did not possess any special financial engineering skills, rather, they applied routine customer facing banking skills to set up and self-authorize fake bank and credit card accounts. It is apparent that investment banks, faced with increasing regulation in the investment banking sphere, have been turning to retail and private banking as alternative sources of revenue. Even Goldman Sachs has established a unit for online personal banking so it may be that this Wells Fargo incident is the first of a new emerging class of risk. It is clear at least that the regulations and procedures put in place by compliance and risk management were not adequate to address this risk at Wells Fargo.

At the same time, it is also the case that banks have been able to put in place many sensible and effective controls to mitigate risks that they do run from their sheer size and complexity. Some of this has come about from the pressure that they have been put under by regulators. A friend of mine is an MD who works in an area called *model risk* at one of the major investment banks on Wall Street.[7] Under the constant prodding of regulators and internal audit, he has constructed a complex set of controls over the various models used by the bank to value every single complex position that is traded there.

If a trader is ever tempted to modify the way a position he is trading is valued, to perhaps help it reflect a profit to his greater advantage, it will be known straight away by those monitoring the valuation models. However, the separation of controls put in place most likely means that the trader, who in prior years would have been able to easily do such a thing, is now not able to do so. While this makes the bank safer than it was, there may be diminishing returns and unintended consequences from further nit picking by regulators with what has been accomplished.

Added regulations and administration has meant the need for banks to add significant resources to meet these regulatory requirements while hamstringing them in other ways. The ban or severe restriction on proprietary trading, the Volcker Rule[8] for example, arguably has already had some negative consequences, even though the ban has only recently come into effect. One unintended consequence is that as banks have been adding to the ranks of staff engaged in compliance matters while they have been losing and shedding the trading talent that has been the long-term source of their competitive advantage. Traders and risk managers have been leaving to join hedge funds, asset managers, and even insurance companies in droves. This drain on talent, has only added to the difficulties banks face in managing their trading risks effectively.

This is some of the context for the operational threats faced by the Banking and financial services industry today. Some of these are posed from the outside, some from the inside. What the banking industry cannot do is afford to let these threats subsist alongside their business model. Rather they have to address the issues head on. We will explore in the succeeding chapters how some of the changes described here have led to these threats and some of the tools that firms can leverage to address them successfully. We now turn our attention to some of these major events and losses.

Notes

1. According to the first shareowner census undertaken by the New York Stock Exchange (NYSE) in 1952, only 6.5 million Americans owned common stock (about 4.2 percent of the US population). By 1990, the NYSE census revealed that more than 51 million Americans owned stocks—more than 20 percent of the US population.

2. In the 1960s, finance's share of the GDP accounted for less than 5 percent of the US economy's output. By the 2000s, the proportion had risen to over 8 percent, fueled by a combination of middleman fees, for example, in asset management, and the credit explosion fueled by securitization (more of that later). The repeal of Glass-Steagall enabled large banks to take advantage of these secular trends and bulk up through acquisition to provide services across the whole range of banking services, including retail, wholesale, asset management, treasury services, etc. Banking balance sheets of over $2 trillion came into being in the 2000s.

3. As interim Assistant Secretary of the Treasury for Financial Stability from October 2008 to May 2009, Neel Kashkari oversaw the Troubled Asset Relief Program (TARP) that was a major component of the US government's response to the financial crisis of 2007. Subsequently, as Chief of the Federal Reserve Bank of Minneapolis he has been an outspoken proponent of further reforms to manage risks posed by large banks. His most recent proposals made in November 2016 were covered widely by the press, including the article reference below: http://www.reuters.com/article/us-usa-fed-kashkari-idUSKBN13B1LD.

4. JP Morgan Chase agreed to pay $1.7 billion as part of a deferred prosecution agreement reached with the US Attorney's office for the Southern District of New York in January 2014 on charges that its failure to maintain an effective anti-money laundering program helped to facilitate the multi-billion-dollar Ponzi scheme orchestrated by Bernard Madoff. The crux of the complaint by federal prosecutors was that the bank maintained the relationship despite internal concerns and red flags. These red flags were actually raised by the London Branch with the UK's Serious Organized Crime Agency but were not shared with the AML Compliance team in the United States. Whether that was because of misplaced concerns over potential noncompliance with data privacy laws in the UK if such client concerns were raised in another country is a troubling possibility. Be that as it may, much work has been done since then, to improve the AML program at JP Morgan Chase, including significant investment in systems and expertise. Information on these charges was reported widely and a good analysis can be found at the link to a DealBook NY Times article: https://dealbook.nytimes.com/2014/01/07/jpmorgan-settles-with-federal-authorities-in-madoff-case/.

5. A credit default swap (CDS) is a financial swap agreement that the seller of the CDS will compensate the buyer (usually the creditor of the reference loan) in the event of a loan default (by the debtor) or other credit event. This is to say that the seller of the CDS insures the buyer against some reference loan defaulting. The buyer of the CDS makes a series of payments (the CDS "fee" or "spread") to the seller and, in exchange, receives a payoff if the loan defaults. It was invented by Blythe Masters from JP Morgan in 1994. By the end of 2007, the outstanding CDS amount was $62.2 trillion, falling to $26.3 trillion by mid-year 2010 and reportedly

$25.5 trillion in early 2012. CDSs are not traded on an exchange and there is no required reporting of transactions to a government agency.

6. A good overview of the Wells Fargo scandal can be found at a number of sources. One good overview can be found at the Guardian newspaper web site: https:// www.theguardian.com/business/us-money-blog/2016/oct/07/wellsfargo-banking-scandal-financial-crisis.

7. In finance, *model risk* is the *risk* of loss resulting from using models to make decisions, initially and frequently in the context of valuing financial securities. Losses can stem from not having the key data inputs, incorrect calculations and algorithms, inappropriate calibration of the model, and so on.

8. The rule disallowing proprietary trading was credited to former chairman of the Federal Reserve Paul Volcker. In the light of the 2008 Financial Crisis, Mr. Volcker believed that one of the causes of the crisis was the ability of investment banks to deploy the capital of customers in pursuit of speculative and risky trades. The objective of the Volcker Rule then was to prevent such activity in the future.

CHAPTER 2

The Rogue Trader

The Rogue Trader is possibly the most famous in the Pantheon of Rogues of Wall Street. Over the years, there have been two types of Rogue trader: the one who blows up the firm in a sudden frenzy of wild trading activity and the one who acts with slow, steady accumulation of risk, unbeknownst to firm's management.

Rochdale Securities, a once stable, small, firm in Connecticut, was taken out by a single trade in 2012 and so fits into the first category of a sudden burst of wild trading activity.[1] Though the size of the loss was one of the smallest rogue trading episodes we have seen, $5 million in losses, its impact was devastating for Rochdale, which was subsequently forced to close. On the other hand, in 2011, UBS suffered far larger losses resulting from a Rogue Trader who slowly and steadily accumulated a huge level of risk, apparently unbeknownst to senior management. Like the Societe Generale episode before it,[2] the Kweku Adeboli incident (see below) shook up the world of investment banks. "Could it happen here?" boards immediately wanted to know and they asked their chief executive officers. CEOs didn't know, so they, in turn, asked their chief risk officers. Their CROs didn't know so they asked their heads of operational risk. The heads didn't know so they asked their operational risk coverage officers. At that point, the question had probably already been answered in the negative back to the board so it probably didn't matter what the truth was. But the truth is, nobody knows where such an incident will happen again. The only thing that is known is that it will happen again somewhere.

Who Is the Rogue Trader?

So who exactly is the Rogue Trader, and what is the source of his roguishness? He is not the handsome rogue of your Victorian novel. Though he may be handsome, he probably won't want to attract undue attention to his activities. He is more likely to be the rat creeping around in your sewers, finding a home in the mess and dirt that never gets cleaned up. The profile of the Rogue Trader is fairly consistent: male, early thirties, not the most favored by birth or schooling. He likely has a strong sense of his abilities and is also likely to underestimate those of his better-educated, more high-born colleagues. More importantly, he is likely also to underestimate the risks of trading without active supervision. It certainly takes a good deal of self-confidence to take on all the risks that the Rogue Trader takes on. Much of that self-confidence is likely fueled by a bull market and a lack of experience and understanding of how markets can suddenly change to the negative. Like many traders, the Rogue Trader will tend to attribute his success to his brilliance rather than the market. Unlike other traders, however, he has no supervisors or colleagues to protect and help him when the market changes, because he does everything in secret.

Generally, the Rogue Trader is not a direct entrant into the bank's trading team but came to it via a role in operations or the back office. Nor does he generally work in the most prestigious or complex areas of trading. More likely, he is part of a team that facilitates fairly routine types of trades for institutional clients. In the stand-out cases such as Societe Generale, Barings,[3] and UBS, the Rogue Trader has been distinguished by his operational knowhow and his aggressive approach. However, such attributes do not necessarily set him obviously apart from his colleagues. Moreover, such aggressiveness is likely to bring plaudits rather than suspicion from his manager. Kweku Adoboli, for example, was reported to have participated in sports betting on the side, and was evidently warned against such activity by compliance. Such activity could potentially have been a red flag. However, for those who have read *Liars Poker*[4] and read about the card-playing exploits of investment bank executives like James Cayne,[5] such activity did not obviously stand out on the trading floor. In fact, it may be that supervisors would have seen this as an indication of the type of aggressive trading activity they were looking for in their young traders.

Indeed, after working for two years as a trading analyst in the bank's back office, Adoboli was promoted to a Delta One trading desk. In 2008, he became a director on the ETF desk, and by 2010, he was promoted to director, with a total annual salary of almost £200,000 (about $254,000). Beginning in 2008, Adoboli started using the bank's money for unauthorized trades. He entered false information into UBS's computers to hide the risky trades he was making. He exceeded the bank's per-employee daily trading limit of $100 million, and failed to hedge his trades against risk. In mid-2011, UBS launched an internal investigation into Adoboli's trades. On September 14, 2011, Adoboli wrote an email to his manager admitting to booking false trades. His trades cost the bank $2 billion (£1.3 billion) and wiped off $4.5 billion (£2.7 billion) from its share price. The trading losses he incurred while trading for his bank were the largest unauthorized trading losses in British history.

In other respects, Kweku Adoboli fitted the classic Rogue Trader profile to a tee. Being from Nigeria, he was clearly not from the classic Oxbridge, upper-class English background favored by English investment banks. For his bachelor's degree, Adoboli went to Nottingham Polytechnic and studied computer science rather than Classics. He joined UBS in an operations role and was later able to cross over to a trading role on the Delta One Desk,[6] where he facilitated large client equity trades. He lived in an up-market part of London and his work financed an expensive lifestyle. He was living the dream. Looking at Adoboli's profile in retrospect, one may wonder why he didn't stand out more from his colleagues. In reality, however, many of Adoboli's colleagues likely shared several aspects of this profile: his age, sex, lifestyle, and the aggressive, hard-charging trading and work ethic. Slightly more unusual was his educational and work background in operations. However, it is the content of what Adoboli did at work, of course, that truly distinguished him from his colleagues. This is where any detective work should have come in. The fact that he was able to succeed in his deception for so long—some three years—highlights the difficulties involved in identifying such illicit activities.

The Crime of Rogue Trading

So what exactly is the Rogue Trader's sin? Traders are clearly paid by their employers to take risks. What exactly is wrong with the risks that the Rogue Trader takes?

Simply put, trading floors require traders to be supervised. Rogue Traders do everything they can to evade supervision. Rogue Traders tend to operate on trading desks responsible for facilitating client trades and, as such, are generally barred from taking risks with their own trades. Their clients tend to include institutions such as asset managers that buy and sell stock in bulk. A client may, for example, want to sell $1 billion worth of stock in a certain company. The job of the trader is to achieve the best price for his client. This requires speed and secrecy to prevent buyers from bidding the price down once they become aware of the seller. Clients pay their bankers large fees to make sure this happens. As a result, at a large investment bank, trading books of some of the traders working in institutional equities can be in the billions of dollars buying and selling the stocks in which they make a market for their customers. For such traders, there are huge levels of potential risk unless their positions are hedged—that is, matching of long positions (loss in market value hurts them) with short positions (loss in market value helps them) in equal amounts. Profit comes, then, not from changes in market values—they should be market neutral—but from the commissions and financing fees from the large trades they execute. Such traders are not supposed to make a lot of money in betting on the direction of a particular stock or group of stocks. There is too much risk involved for that.

In addition, in a typical investment bank, traders are generally limited to trading securities strictly within the scope of their "trading mandate." An equity trader's mandate should be generally restricted to trading equities, a fixed income trader to certain fixed income products, and so on. A broad mandate is then defined down to a specific set of limits that a trader should trade within in order to restrict the potential losses that can be suffered from his book on any given day. This is called his VaR (value-at-risk) limit.[7]

Without limit management, given the number of traders and the size of their trading books in a large investment bank, banks potentially face catastrophic losses on any given day. Limits tend to be defined based on the level of experience and seniority of the trader and act to limit the potential size of a trader's profit for a day, a week, or a year, as well as his potential loss. Any trader who wishes to increase his profit opportunity can theoretically do so by increasing or exceeding his trading limits. While a Genius Trader may prevail upon management to assent to a temporary or permanent limit increase because he or she is a genius (discussed further in Chapter 3), no such privileges are likely to be extended to ordinary folk, the ranks of which are populated by the potential Rogue Trader. Such a trader will only be able to exceed his trade limits by deception—in other words, without authorization. He does this by various illegal methods of falsification and wrongful concealment of his tracks and activities. One can now see why this is such a serious offense and why it is labeled rogue trading. No trading operation can survive without defining such limits and requiring traders to stay within them unless otherwise authorized to do so. Trading without authorization is the source of the Rogue Trader's crime and is punishable with jail time, depending on the extent of the losses he causes to his employer. These can be very large when things go badly wrong because he is trading unsupervised as well as unauthorized.

Tools of the Rogue Trader's Trade

A trader seeking larger profit opportunities has to exceed his limits without seeming to—that is, through various means of deception. The basic objective is always to make sure that the trading book does not cause any unusual questions to be asked by supervisors, controllers, and limit checkers. In general this means making it appear that the trader's positions and risk levels are reasonably well hedged in line with expectations and prescribed limits. There are many tricks that may be employed in order to do this. Here are just a few that have been identified.

Intraday Trading

One opportunity traders on occasion take advantage of is the fact that their trading limits are generally set for the end of the trading day rather than intraday. The reason for this is simple: At the end of day, traders' positions are closed and static and therefore easily measurable. During the day, however, positions are constantly being updated and changed to reflect active trades and other transaction data. As a result, traders may execute trades in excess of their end-of-day limit during the trading day, either intentionally or unintentionally. As long as traders are able to bring their positions back down by day-end, any intraday position excesses are normally unexamined. A deliberate strategy to trade beyond a trader's end-of-day limits by a considerable amount intraday is not necessarily easy to catch for the reasons just discussed. Furthermore, it is arguable, and has been argued by risk managers, that since the limit is an end-of-day limit, trading beyond it during the day is neither illegal nor unauthorized. While difficult to catch and prove, the extent of any loss is limited to those that can accumulate in a single day, which of course can be in the millions.

Phantom Trades

Another strategy a trader may employ is to modify the trading book prior to the supervisory and controller review at the end of the trading day (supervisors are expected generally to review trader activity at the end of the day). This can be done by creating nonexistent trades to balance out the real trades. Subsequent to the reviews, the trader cancels out the nonexistent trades and repeats such activities on a nightly basis.

Fake Counterparties

Another strategy has been to create fake counterparties to trade with, thereby allowing fictitious trades with that counterparty to be entered into his trading book to balance out the real trades. In all these cases, the trader creates an illusion of a hedged book. In reality, the book is anything but hedged.

Slush Fund

In order to allow such a strategy to work over a period of time, the trader needs to keep undue attention away from himself. He is thus likely to use a secret account that enables smoothing of profits over time so neither profits nor losses are overly excessive. Excess profits may be transferred to the secret "slush fund" account on good days and transferred back to the trading account on bad days. The creation and use of such accounts was a key point discussed at the trial of Kweku Adoboli. Such accounts normally can be created fairly easily though it may require controllers' help (knowingly or unknowingly) to evade their detection.

Developing expertise in or gaining access to back-office systems in order to evade them then is a core part of the Rogue Trader's skill set. However, as we saw with the Rochdale case, a trader can sometimes do untold harm with one trade that gets through the system, which is well beyond the limits that can be borne by the firm. A small firm can have zero tolerance for such fatal trades whereas a large investment bank or hedge fund has most to fear from the type of rogue trading that took place at UBS.

How Rogue Traders Succeed

With gatekeepers at every step in the process of trade execution—supervisors, controllers, operations, counterparty operations—one might think that to elude them all is some sort of magic feat. While there is certainly some skill involved, it is not magic but a couple of crucial factors that enable some Rogue Traders to escape detection for so long (see Table 2-1).

First is the incentive structure still in place at investment banks. Traders' compensation has traditionally been binary and asymmetric, rewarding profit taking without punishment for losses and risky activities. Too often, management looks the other way to reward profits from risky trades. This is short-sighted. As history has shown, the winning trades of today are often the huge losses of tomorrow. Second is the problem of not big but "mega data." Banks are drowning in data. Millions of trades are executed every day at the major investment banks. Even a small percentage of exceptions—trades that are can-celed or corrected—is a few thousand on a daily basis, and so it is next to impossible to find the cancels and corrects of the Rogue Trader amongst the normal, regular, and benign flow of business corrections. In a similar vein, large investment banks trade with hundreds of counterparties; if one is ficti-tious, it will be very hard to find. Yet both these problems have their corollary in solutions.

Can the Rogue Trader Be Stopped?

It is likely impossible to completely stop Rogue Traders. What firms should aim for is minimizing the period of time such activity can go undetected and minimizing the extent of the losses.

Table 2-1 Infamous Rogue Traders

Trader	Year	Loss (in US billions)	Firm	Years Undetected
Kweku Adoboli	2011	~$2.3	UBS	At least 3
Jerome Kerviel	2007	~$7.2	Societe General	At least 3
Nick Leeson	1995	~$2	Barings	At least 3

First, incentive structures for traders should be reexamined. The practice of banks rewarding employees for risky trading activity should be eliminated. Instead, firms need to continue to reshape their culture to reflect the change in business strategy in the post–Dodd-Frank world,[8] which includes changing incentive structures. This includes, for example, deploying clawbacks[9] on traders "swinging the bat" or making profits for trades in breach of agreed limits or outside the scope of their mandate. Additionally, incentive structures for traders whose job is to facilitate client trades rather than trade on the bank's own account, increasingly the norm in investment banks, should reflect their client relationship management objectives more clearly. Such incentive structures should reflect effective risk management and reward good citizenship. For example, traders identifying opportunities to improve the control environment or alerting management to risky behaviors on the floor, as well as delivering excellent client relationship management results, can be incentivized.

Second, trading systems and controls should be redesigned to reflect this change in culture and objectives. Investment bank systems have traditionally put traders at their logical center, maximizing features such as flexibility to allow traders to enter new clients and trades while bypassing certain controls. System design priorities in a Dodd-Frank world need to reflect the twin priorities of clients and risk management. Putting clients and risk at the system's core enables management to organically track client limits and conflicts across the bank's business portfolio. Better understanding client needs and profitability across the platform—M&A advisory, lending, underwriting, asset and wealth management, sales, and trading—should also follow, and this will help to grow the business as well as manage risk more effectively.

Third, banks should review their fraud detection methods and procedures. Big data can be the solution as well as the problem. It is clear from publicly available reports that Rogue Traders have been able to conceal their activities for several years at banks with, on the face of it at least, fairly well-established operational risk functions and controls. It would seem, then, that more aggressive or more precise methods are called for. Retail banks and insurance companies have typically established dedicated fraud units and antifraud software to fight insurance fraud, cybercrime, and other types of fraud. Such methods are worth exploring in the investment-banking world. Harnessing technology is, of course, already a big part of anti–rogue trading programs in investment banks in the form of trade surveillance, automated trade reconciliation, cancel and correct monitoring, and so on. Given the vast amount of data, however, in these different areas it is not clear how effective such tools can be on a one-off basis in identifying suspicious activities. Algorithmic data mining and big data analysis could potentially be very useful in helping banks to connect the dots. Take, for example, a trader with several personal trading policy violations. Perhaps, on their own, these might not be sufficient to warrant any special investigation. But were this same trader also identified as someone who had moved from operations to the front office, had not taken mandatory leave,[10] and had also accumulated unusual levels of trading profit on a client facilitation desk, such a combination might easily make the trader a candidate for a deep-dive investigation. In the large and complex world of the modern investment bank, such triggers can probably only be pulled with applications based on investment in intelligent and natural learning. Figure 2-1 highlights some of these indicators.

Fourth, banks need to continuously review the checks and balances established to prevent and mitigate rogue trading behaviors. Many banks did just

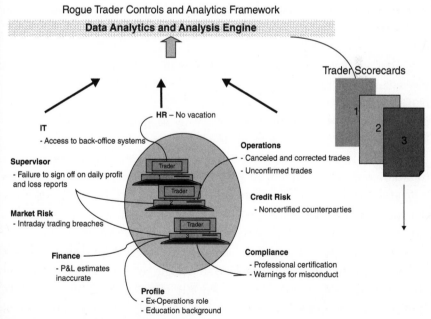

Figure 2-1: Indicators of Rogue Trader risk

this in the wake of the recent UBS/Adoboli incident in 2011. The key checks include, inter alia:

- Mandatory vacation policy—this was introduced in investment banks to ensure the ability of supervisors to independently take a look at every traders' book during their annual leave, something that never happened with Kerviel at Societe Generale.
- System entitlements—traders should not be entitled to edit operational systems, as this could be a way for them to manage their back-office accounting.
- Segregation of duties—there should be clear separation of duties between traders, operations, and accounting to ensure that traders are not in a position to manipulate their accounts, confirmations records, etc.
- Trade-limit monitoring—a separate risk management function should be reviewing trade limits and ensuring that traders stay within theirs.
- Independent valuation and profit and loss reviews—traders should not provide the valuation of their trades and position; there should be an independent function doing so.
- Confirmation procedures—banks should make sure there are independent confirmation procedures to ensure that the bank is able to verify that the traders' trades are genuine.

Technology has a big part to play in making such reviews effective and efficient. Consider system entitlements, for example. Investment banks today deploy so many systems, and within these systems, so many different roles and responsibilities, that without specifically designed tools and intelligent automation, it is impossible to track whether an individual has the system entitlements needed to do his or her job. In such an environment, without well-designed exception tracking and reporting, it is easy to see how an individual could accumulate entitlements to systems that will help support a scheme with nefarious objectives.

In summary, the controls against rogue trading in an investment bank comprise a combination of cultural change and intelligent or cognitive system reengineering. It is likely impossible to stop Rogue Traders altogether, but significantly reducing the duration of undetected periods of activity and the size of the consequent losses is a reasonable objective. Executing the strategies discussed here to transform the culture and technology of investment banks will help support the achievement of that goal.

Notes

1. Rochdale Securities was a brokerage firm that went bankrupt in 2012 due to a loss on a single trade that was executed. The failure came since the trade's losses were beyond the capacity of the firm to meet.

2. In 2009, Societe Generale lost over $7 billion due to the activities of trader Jerome Kerviel. This remains the largest-ever loss resulting from a Rogue Trader. One of the tactics used by Kerviel to avoid detection was to create false counterparties that would then be used to authenticate his nefarious trades.

3. In many ways the original Rogue Trader, Nick Leeson managed to bring down the storied Barings Investment Bank all on his own. In the early 1990s, Leeson was able to take advantage of his role as head of operations and trading in a satellite trading unit in Hong Kong to take on huge, unhedged positions that resulted ultimately in a spectacular loss for the bank.

4. *Liars Poker* by Michael Lewis chronicled his adventures as a securities salesman at Salomon Brothers in the early 1980s. The title of the book comes from the poker game that was played on the trading floor. Trading heads were in many cases the instigators of the games, a sine qua non for success in trading.

5. James Cayne, known widely as Jimmy, was the CEO of Bear Stearns in the years leading up to the 2008 Financial Crisis. He gained some notoriety in the press for his publicized participation in bridge tournaments during some tough times for his company.

6. Delta One is the name for the trading desk on investment banking trading floors for some of the more straightforward equity trading activities. Delta One is so known because of the one-to-one relationship between the trades and swaps being executed on behalf of clients.

7. VaR (value at risk) is the term given to risk-management modeling methodologies developed in investment banks. The models developed under this methodology are intended to indicate the amount of value that would be lost in a day under given trading scenarios. The scenarios are normally developed on the basis of historical precedent.

8. Dodd-Frank Act is the name for legislation passed following the 2008 Financial Crisis. Christopher Dodd and Barney Frank were the congressmen responsible for the legislation. One of the most expensive pieces of financial legislation ever passed, its intention was to prevent a recurrence of the type of financial failures that were perceived to be the underlying causes of the 2008 Financial Crisis and the deep recession that followed.

9. *Clawback* is the term used in investment banking to refer to the provision to take back bonuses previously paid out to traders if certain conditions are met. The most

frequent of these conditions are if any part of the bonus was paid on the basis of trades that were incorrectly or inappropriately executed.

10. In the Societe Generale incident in 2009, Kerviel worked through his vacations because he did not want anyone to look into his trading book, something that could have happened if he had gone on vacation. Following the incident, investment banks instituted mandatory vacations to prevent such a recurrence.

CHAPTER 3

Genius Traders: Who They Are and How to Catch Them

Whereas the Rogue Trader operates behind the scenes and needs must remain hidden, the Genius Trader upends things while operating in plain view. When the Genius Trader strikes, it is not, strictly speaking, a case of trader malfeasance but of trader overreach spurred on by ego, enthusiastic management support, and, as a result, a lack of tight controls.

Characteristics of the Genius Trader

The Genius Trader is not as well known to the general public as his cousin the Rogue Trader, but the threat he poses to investment banks, their employees, and their shareholders is just as real. Who exactly is he? Well, he is a genius, of course. Furthermore, he is head over heels in love with his own genius, and so is everyone around him. He does not need to work behind the scenes like the Rogue Trader to gain access to large amounts of capital to trade with. Instead he works in the open with the full support of management.

Aside from being unusually smart and intellectually confident, what else distinguishes a Genius Trader? After all, being super smart and intellectually confident describes many traders at investment banks or hedge funds. In addition, then, Genius Traders have acquired during their tenure, or come to the bank with, an almost unimpeachable reputation for trading success. That success more often than not has resulted from exotic and obscure trades that netted significant profits for the firm. Even better if such profits were won in a trading cycle that was tough to do well in, and were achieved by taking positions contra to the general market sentiment. Such a label applies, for example, to a John Paulson[1] or a Steve Eisman,[2] each of whom made huge profits on bets contrary to the housing bubble in 2007. Such success is often associated with genius and the perceived rare ability to succeed in any market circumstances. While there is no guarantee that such insight will lead to repeat success in the future, such results are often hailed as if they do and lead those around the "genius" to loosen the grip of controls that would normally be exercised.

Another feature of a Genius Trader and the environment he operates in are frequent overrides of standards and procedures that are applied to all others. Two of those areas are worth dwelling on a little: trading limits and valuation policies. Generally speaking, one important aspect of trading risk management is to ensure that the exposure to any one particular product, region, trader, or counterparty is limited to a certain level of potential losses. This is done by applying a fixed limit to the size of positions that can be taken with respect to any single product, geographic region, trader and trading desk, and trading counterparty. By setting such limits, the bank can contain the losses from a trading strategy that finds itself on the wrong side of the market. While typically such limits are applied in a consistent way to every trader, according to his or her level and experience, one finds that Genius Traders are on occasion given greater latitude. They may, for instance, request a temporary increase in the limit in the size of position they can take because of a specific opportunity that only they know about or that their trading desk is uniquely positioned to take advantage of.

In terms of valuations, such traders are often engaged in trading securities that are hard to value, and as a result can be given latitude to value such positions themselves or to employ different valuation models than are employed elsewhere in the bank. This can give rise to gray and ambiguous positions with the potential opportunity to hide losses without straying outside of any legal boundary. The danger to the bank is that such losses can build on large positions without being brought to the attention of management if the valuation basis is modified to reduce the impact of the losses.

In all of these cases, we should note that the Genius Trader abrogates to himself, by intellectual authority rather than by dissembling, rights and privileges not available to others. This is the key difference with the Rogue Trader. It is also the case that such a Genius Trader sometimes occupies positions in the highest level of their bank or firm and is given honor and respect of the most senior members of the firm.

Genius Trader risk is also distinguished by the fact that people appear to be generally prepared to overlook missteps. A well-known example of genius, perhaps the classic example, is John Meriwether,[3] the trader who left Salomon Brothers to establish the hedge fund Long Term Capital. After the infamous losses and then the closure of Long Term Capital, Meriwether succeeded in growing a second fund, JWM Partners, until on July 7, 2009, it was announced that the fund would close after suffering losses. A third fund was then started in 2010 with some large losses announced as early as the following year. Such second and third chances are in strong contrast to Rogue Traders, clearly, whose next occupation is generally that of prison inmate.

A caveat to all of this is that a sharp intellect and high level of proficiency with quantitative techniques and advanced mathematics are prerequisites for good traders. Creativity is also a very important asset in a trader to ensure that they are constantly adapting their trading strategies based on their analysis of changing events in the markets in ways that help to maximize opportunities for themselves and their clients. What sets the Genius Trader apart are these other factors related to a dangerous kind of arrogance that makes him a potential danger to a firm and broader sets of actors.

It is interesting to review the list of the biggest trading losses incurred by individual traders, with the largest losses from Rogue Traders unauthorized by management, and therefore illegal, and the second set from Genius Traders legally made with the apparent full knowledge of management and the risk right in front of them. The losses in the latter group, shown in Table 3-1, are distinguished from the first group, primarily in terms of the size of the losses. Table 3-1 shows that four out of the five largest recorded losses by a single trader were incurred by "Genius Trader Risk," the term I have used to describe the type of risk this second category represents. This is in some ways counterintuitive. Most of the focus around unexpected trading losses has tended to be on Rogue Traders, but the largest losses have come from the risk right in front of you, traders operating with the full support of management. Table 3-1 shows five separate incidents with losses of over $5 billion where only one was perpetrated by a Rogue Trader. After the loss incurred by Jerome Kerviel, the next largest loss from a Rogue

Table 3-1 Trading Losses

Trader	Type	Year	Loss (in US billions)	Next Position
Bruno Iksil	Genius	2012	~$7*	TBD
Howie Hubler	Genius	2007	~$9	Loan Value Group
Jerome Kerviel	Rogue	2007	~$7	Jail
Brian Hunter	Genius	2005	~$6 to $7	Peak Ridge Capital
John Meriwether	Genius	1998	~$5 to 6	JWM Partners

*Loss includes payment of $920 million made by JP Morgan to regulators in the US and the UK.

Trader event was that by Kweku Adoboli at UBS in 2011, which saw a loss of some $2.3 billion.

One reason for the disparity in size between losses that have resulted from genius trading risk versus rogue trading risk is because it is not so easy for a Rogue Trader to hide large positions from management. Losses tend to mount in an unhedged position so that at some point, these losses become apparent to someone, a controller for instance or a trading supervisor. Most investment banks have a certain number of small rogue trading incidents each year—incidents that are too small to become the subject of media coverage or regulatory concern. On the other hand, Genius Traders tend to be given latitude to trade, meaning large amounts of capital to trade with, and so the losses correspondingly will be higher when the market moves against them. There are also a large number of losses made by Genius Traders each year, too. However, it is rare that they are labeled as operational risk incidents—in other words, incidents caused by an operational failure.[4] Maybe they will be called market risk incidents—the market simply went against the trader's position. Whether or not they are labeled as operational failures, of course, does not matter. What does matter is that there are indicators of this risk that can be tracked the way the diagram in Figure 3-1 shows.

The key indicators and controls against Genius Traders are:

- Exception processing—the trader requires exceptions to be made for the way his books are valued, perhaps not by the standard models.
- Supervision—the supervisor has difficulties understanding the trades executed and the strategy behind them.

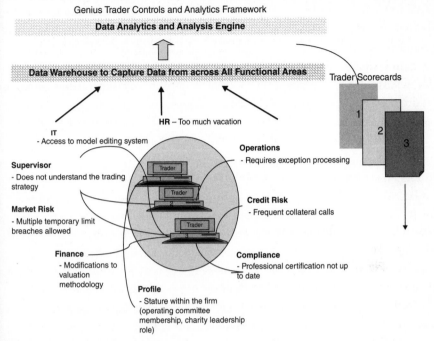

Figure 3-1: Indicators of genius risk

- Trade limit breaches—trade limit breaches by the trader are frequent, and exceptions are granted on a regular basis.
- Stature within the firm—the trader's stature within the firm is such that he is untouchable.
- Trades in complex and hard-to-value securities—the trader plies his trade in securities that are obscure to the firm and hard to value. Generally used valuation processes tend to be replaced by custom spreadsheets managed by the trader's team, leading potentially to suspension of separation of duties between the independent valuation team and the trading team.

How to Manage Genius Risk

So now that we know how to identify genius risk, how can banks do a better job managing it?

First, senior management must regard "genius" with a critical eye and in the context of the "best interests of the team." An example from soccer can be instructive here. Sir Alex Ferguson, ex-coach of Manchester United, over the years showed the door to top stars like Carlos Tevez, Christian Ronaldo, and David Beckham when their egos threatened the team's overall stability. Such stars demand privilege and latitude that may result in negative consequences for the overall health of the team.[5] As that example nicely illustrates, a manager and an institution's culture can be more successful when it is stronger and more confident than its biggest egos. Managers should have very limited tolerance for exceptions and individuals not willing to play as part of a team.

Second, banks can use data to expose the objective reality of different traders' performance. Another example from sports is useful here. Coaches in baseball, memorably portrayed in Michael Lewis's book and the film made of it, *Moneyball*,[6] have mined data to expose when long-held views about the value of certain types of players do not coincide with the reality. Mining financial trade data could be done to challenge similarly held views about the value and consistency of different traders. It is possible that a trader's reputation for brilliance on the back of several risky and very successful trades would not be borne out on the basis of longer-run statistical analysis. To counter such perception with objective data might help to reverse decisions to extend more latitude to such traders, the sort of latitude that led to the sorts of disasters we have just discussed.

Third, it may well be worthwhile employing such people provided management does not allow them the latitude they might seek. While it is always useful to have bright people round, management needs to keep them in the team and playing by team rules. If management is not strong enough to enforce such rules or the trader does not or cannot comply, then such traders have to be shown the door.

Fourth, objective data analysis should also be used to identify certain patterns of behavior that might be suggestive of greater risk taking by certain traders if left unchallenged. Such type of analysis to catch a Genius Trader might include, for example, failures to document trade activities per requirements; routine requests to exceed trading limits temporarily; and changes in core valuation methodologies[7] because they no longer represent market realities. The analysis of such exceptions in an analytical framework might support the targeting of such traders more effectively.

Fifth, there is potential here to leverage machine-learning applications to identify when such indicators are present in the trading environment. Systematic surveillance of traders to identify norms of activity vis-à-vis these indicators should be helpful in identifying correlation of anomalous activities, and whether or not they present true exceptions and potentially risky behavior. We will explore these types of trade surveillance activities in Chapter 21.

Finally, if you are ever presented with an opportunity to invest with or take on a Genius Trader who has suffered a misstep, don't take it. The chances are that she or he will blow up again.

Notes

1. John Paulson was featured in the book *The Greatest Trade Ever* by Gregory Zuckerman. In 2006, the middle-aged hedge fund manager John Paulson seemed to be falling behind his young competitors, who were all reaping the benefits of the real estate boom and subprime mortgages. Then, with the aid of his analyst Paolo Pellegrini, Paulson became convinced that the housing market was headed for a crash, and defied conventional wisdom by betting heavily on obscure bearish trades. Few banks or investors would invest in his new fund, and many accused him of rash counterintuitiveness, but Paulson persevered and steadily bet "against the house." In 2007 his firm made $15 billion, one of the greatest financial trades of all time. The story is well told in this book about the trade.

2. Michael Lewis, *The Big Short: Inside the Doomsday Machine* (New York: W. W. Norton & Company, 2010). Steve Eisman was featured in *The Big Short*. The book was about several of the key players in the creation of the credit default swap market that sought to bet against the collateralized debt obligation (CDO) bubble and thus ended up profiting from the financial crisis of 2007–2010.

3. Michael Lewis, *Liar's Poker* (New York: W. W. Norton & Company, 2010). John Meriwether was a noted bond trader at Salomon Brothers in the early 1980s and was a leading character in the book. He left Salomon Brothers in 1991 and founded Long Term Capital in 1993, a hedge fund leveraging people and trading ideas that he had worked on at Salomons.

4. Operational risk incidents are losses that occur to firms as a result of operational errors and flaws. Under Basel II, investment banks and other financial entities are required to keep track of such incidents and ensure that they model the losses that can occur from such incidents to ensure capital is set aside in the event that they reoccur.

5. Alex Ferguson: My Autobiography.

6. Michael Lewis, *Moneyball* (New York: W. W. Norton & Company, 2004). *Moneyball*, later adapted as a movie, described the innovations from the use of statistical methods to analyze the performance of different players in baseball. The result of the

analysis undercut the prevailing ways of thinking about what constituted the most valuable types of players to the success of a baseball team.

7. Valuation methodologies—Investment banks are required to ensure consistent and accurate methodologies are applied to value each of the security positions their traders hold. Typically independent controllers check that such methodologies meet the required criteria. When traders are given license to override such agreed on approaches, the danger is that they then have latitude to value positions in ways that favor them.

CHAPTER 4

Insider Trading

I nsider trading has long been at the core of any definition of operational and trading risks against which an entity must defend itself. The rapid spread of hedge funds and the ultra-competitiveness of their traders has only increased the need for vigilance in this area. Significant and widespread prosecution of the crime suggests that more can be done by the industry to manage the issue. But what can be done? To paraphrase Sigmund Freud, understanding the problem will go a long way toward solving it.

What Is Insider Trading

At its most basic, insider trading is just as it sounds: trading on "inside information." In other words, it is trading in a company's stock on the basis of material information that only people inside the company should ideally be privy to. People inside the company are prohibited from trading on such information, as is anyone who happens to come into receipt of it. Such practice has been illegal since the Securities and Exchange Act of 1934. This Act defines corporate insiders as a company's officers, directors, and any beneficial owners of more than 10 percent of a class of the company's equity securities.[1]

In the United States and many other jurisdictions, however, "insiders" are not just limited to corporate insiders where illegal insider trading is concerned but can include any individual who trades shares based on material nonpublic information (MNPI)[2] in violation of a duty of trust. This duty may be imputed; for example, in many jurisdictions, in cases of where a corporate insider "tips" a friend about nonpublic information likely to have an effect on the company's share price, the duty the corporate insider owes the company is now imputed to the friend and the friend violates a duty to the company if he trades on the basis of this information.

The advantage and importance of "good information" in trading is perhaps nowhere better illustrated than by the legend regarding the rise of the House of Rothschild during the Napoleonic Wars. Napoleon was decisively defeated by the combined forces of Britain and Prussia in 1815, but it had been far from a foregone conclusion. The well-known story goes that a carrier pigeon dispatched to London gave Nathan Rothschild this critical information ahead of other traders. This enabled him to take full advantage in currency markets and trading in British government bonds. There was nothing illegal about this but it is not so easy to get a differentiating trading edge like that in markets these days.

Generally speaking, *information* is defined in the Securities and Exchange Act as anything that could have a material bearing on the stock price, such as quarterly results, positive results from research for a new drug, acquisition of a major new client, and improved sales results. A trade to take advantage of such information is executed prior to the public release of that information so that the stock price does not yet reflect it. At the point the information is released to the public, the stock price likely changes to reflect the new information, and so the insider benefits from having bought at a lower or higher (if she shorted the stock, expecting a drop in its price) price point.

A classic example was provided in recent times by that of Rajat Gupta, erstwhile managing partner of McKinsey & Co. and director at Goldman Sachs. In 2012, Gupta was convicted by a federal jury of leaking insider information gained from the boardroom of Goldman Sachs to Raj Rajaratnam—at the time, the head of the Galleon Group. The evidence of trades executed by Galleon in conjunction with phone call evidence ahead of news about Goldman were what paved the way for a successful conviction.[3]

In summary, deliberately trading on inside information is a crime, and legislators and regulators in the United States and other developed economies have built an infrastructure of laws and regulations to try to prevent it. In the United States, elaborate rules and procedures have been defined in the securities industry regulations determining how and when material information is released to the public, what officers can say to outsiders, and when employees can trade in their company's stock, all to ensure that the integrity of the marketplace is maintained. For example, companies release quarterly earnings results after the market closes or prior to the market opening to ensure market participants have the opportunity to digest the information prior to the onset of trading activity.

Although insider trading is sometimes described as a crime without victims, there are actually three sets of victims. First, there are the other investors in the company stock who do not have access to the inside information that the insiders have. Without the benefit of such information, investors may well be induced to sell their stock at a price below its (now) true value to the person who does have the information. This scenario is a bit like a person selling a highly valuable painting at a garage sale. The buyer is an art expert and is aware of the painting's true value but offers only a fraction of the value to the seller who is unaware of the true worth. It is clear that in this scenario, the seller has been "had." The person selling to someone in possession of inside information is the victim of the same kind of unfairness. If the seller knew what the buyer knew, he would not sell at that price.

Second, a broad effect can theoretically occur if investors are led to conclude that the game is rigged, and they may withdraw from the market as a result. This has a negative impact on all those invested in the market. Third, in the case of firms closing (several hedge funds have been forced to do so following insider trading scandals), the folks who work there in operations, accounting, technology, and other departments lose their jobs. The employees of the organization that are forced to close down are often the silent victims.

The Industry of Insider Trading

Unlike, say, dealing in drugs, dealing in inside information is full of gray areas that dealers have been able to take advantage of. Unlike many other crimes, there is some level of ambiguity attached to insider trading that makes going after its traffickers tricky: (1) what exactly constitutes "material nonpublic information" (MNPI); (2) how to determine who is in possession of such information; (3) how to identify those who are trading on it with the requisite intent to do so; and (4) how to determine if the person providing the information benefited from doing so and if the person receiving it was aware of that. Recent court cases have highlighted some of these issues.[4]

However, our purpose here is not to review the legal issues at stake but to analyze the risks that are presented by insider trading cases to the risk manager and compliance officer on the trading floor. Most recently, two types of financial service firms have been prominent in the prosecution of insider trading cases in most recent times: expert networks, which are firms that provide consulting advice to trading firms, and hedge funds.

The middlemen in the insider trading industry are the industry insiders, bankers and expert networks who can (sometimes unknowingly) link the users (traders) to the suppliers (industry executives and researchers—the people with access to inside information). The insider information operation is financed by the users who are willing to pay good rates for the information. The industry is global in its scope. Many of the cases brought have turned on evidence that expert networks and investment bankers provided MNPI to their clients. There are undoubtedly many expert networks that do provide a legitimate service, helping hedge funds and analysts to research an industry and company on the basis of public information. However, there is very little regulation of such companies, and it is easy to see how such legitimate research can turn into passing on inside information.

The inside information industry would not exist without the demand of users. Cases since 2009 have brought low several major and well-established multi-billion-dollar hedge funds, including Galleon Group, SAC Capital, Front Point Partners, Diamondback Capital Management, and New Castle Funds.[5]

So what is it about hedge funds that have given rise to this trend? Hedge funds have grown ever more ubiquitous as more and more traders from large banks, frustrated with red tape and declining pay, have left to set up their own shops. These are typically aggressive types, quite different from the portfolio managers of the more traditional and conservative asset management firms. They tend to build very sleek and streamlined organizations with very little infrastructure. It is not unusual for a young fund to have a billion dollars or more under management, with relatively few staff members in operations and a fairly junior chief financial officer (CFO) or controller. In some cases, hedge funds may take on an experienced CFO to help set up the infrastructure and systems, only to replace him or her with a more junior and lower-paid person once the operation is in place.

A story of an ex-colleague of mine, John, a very experienced hedge fund controller, illustrates this very nicely. John was a hardworker which was good because there was a lot of work to do. He rarely stopped for lunch and usually worked through late evening. When I first met John, I was nominally his boss but after two weeks on the job he still did not know my name. "I'm sorry but who are you again?" He asked when I came over one day to ask him a question. It was not rudeness. He was just too busy. What was his job? To make sure that the huge portfolio of securities he was responsible for were accounted for correctly on a daily basis. It took all of his time and attention. Later in his career, John was appointed CFO by the partners of a new hedge fund in 2010. The partners were former traders at a large investment bank and had no experience in establishing and running a hedge fund and the infrastructure that entails. John set up the systems and infrastructure needed to ensure investor requirements were met, valuations and returns were accurate, and so on. About two years later, the fund had raised over a $1 billion, facilitated in part by the systems and infrastructure established by John. The returns and asset basis were certainly sufficient at this point to provide the partners with a very healthy income. At this point, however, John was fired and replaced with a more junior person with no more than a year's experience. Little explanation was provided. My point in relating this story is to illustrate the little value typically associated with such functions as the CFO by the partners and portfolio managers.

In addition, compliance functions may well be outsourced by hedge funds, and there is likely no independent risk management function or investment committee to speak of. The weakness of the leadership structure on the control side of the house would be fine, of course, if all hedge fund managers had the talents and ethics of a Warren Buffett. That has certainly not been the case, and sometimes those who fall short are tempted to enhance performance by cheating. Weak control functions make them all the more likely to succeed in doing so. Raising the bar in this area would, it is true, raise the cost of entry into the industry. However, while that might penalize a little the great and the good, it would also serve to filter out the bad and the ugly.

Surveys appear to back up this view. One-third of hedge fund professionals have seen illegal trading practices in their offices, according to a survey of 127 hedge fund professionals conducted by the law firm Labaton Sucharow, HedgeWorld, and the Hedge Fund Association in 2013.[6] Nearly half of respondents (46 percent) believe that their competitors engage in illegal activity, while 35 percent say they have personally felt pressure to break rules. Of those surveyed, 30 percent have witnessed "misconduct" in the workplace. While 87 percent said they would report wrongdoing under the protections of the SEC Whistleblower Program and other such programs, at the same time, 29 percent of respondents reported that they might experience retaliation for doing so. Meanwhile 35 percent of respondents reported feeling pressured by their compensation or bonus plan to violate the law or engage in unethical conduct, while 25 percent of respondents reported other pressures. Twenty-eight percent of respondents reported that if leaders of their firm learned that a top performer had engaged in insider trading, they would be unlikely to report the misconduct to law enforcement or regulatory authorities; 13 percent of respondents reported that leaders of their firm would likely ignore the problem. Still another 13 percent said that hedge fund professionals may need to engage in unethical or illegal tactics to be successful, and an equal percentage would commit a crime—insider trading—if they could make a guaranteed $10 million and get away with it. These responses appear consistent with events on the ground.

Trading Floors and Chinese Walls

This is not to say that large investment banks are free of the insider trading habit. However, in a banking environment, the problem often expresses itself differently.

Traders, analysts, and investment bankers work within the broad church that is the modern investment bank. Bankers work on new issuances of equity and debt, they work on mergers and acquisitions, and they provide advisory services to their clients. Their clients include global corporations, private equity funds, and hedge funds. To provide the expertise and competitive edge to their clients, they draw on the services of their analysts to provide strategy overview and forecasts for the industry, as well as insights into the upcoming moves of key players.

Chinese walls are in place to ensure that *deal teams* working in strictly confidential environments do not provide their colleagues on the public trading floor with access to information about their impending deals. Registers of deals are maintained so that bank employees suspend trading in those companies. Make no mistake—these controls are impressive and without a doubt mitigate the risk of insiders passing on MNPI to their colleagues over the wall. A friend of mine runs this system at one of the major banks and over the years it has grown in sophistication and authority. However, there are still gaps and it is hard to monitor how bankers can potentially profit from such information as the advantage they derive from it is not necessarily expressed in a trading transaction, rather, in advisory contracts won or lead player in an underwriting syndicate.

Meanwhile, over on the trading floor, a real temptation exists for traders to take advantage of client orders they are facilitating. *Front-running* is when a firm trades ahead of a customer's large order that is likely to move the market, profiting off the inside knowledge of the impending change in the price. This activity is normally associated with equity trading, but more recently, criminal charges have been made against traders in foreign currencies.[7] While such activity contravenes FINRA rules, since there is no fiduciary responsibility in this case, leveraging MNPI does not constitute an insider trading crime per se. Nevertheless, a bank's reputation would be seriously impacted if clients were to believe that the traders they are bringing their business to are also acting against their interests in executing their trades.

Monitoring traders' conversations and trades is a strong mechanism for identifying such wrongdoing. It can also show the sequencing of traders' conversations with clients ahead of orders, as they pick up their orders, and as they execute trades to meet those orders. Such monitoring can be programmed in such a way to identify cases where bankers on the "deal" side are talking to colleagues on the public trading floor on the other side of the wall, Very sophisticated tools have been identified to show on network diagrams who is talking to whom and who should not be talking to whom. Furthermore, when trades of concern are noted, conversations that have been archived can be pulled to interrogate traders over such concerns.

Raising the Bar

The push for raising the bar seems most likely to come from investors. For a start, one area of focus should be on ensuring greater transparency into hedge funds' investment decision and trading processes. How about, for instance, requiring discussion and then registration of any potentially "material non-public information" with a control group internal to the fund and independent of the trading team? Such a group, of course, is already required at investment banks and at some of the more firmly established hedge funds (voluntarily). Investments and trades can then be cross-checked against the MNPI registry. Additionally, information upon which an investment thesis has been based is reviewed by control and compliance functions (see Figure 4-1). If the thesis is found to be based, in part, on MNPI, then the proposed investments or transactions are pulled.

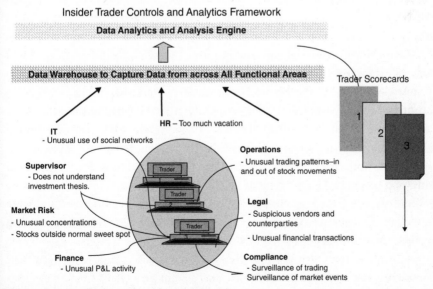

Figure 4-1: Indicators of insider trading risk

Additionally, like at investment banks, an independent compliance function should surveille market events and cross-check in an automated fashion (after the fact) for any trades ahead of those events. This type of control is absolutely standard in investment banks and it should be so also at hedge funds and other asset managers, too. With such controls and surveillance in place, it should be possible to identify trading activity that is potentially based on insider information:

- Observance of unusual trading patterns in and out of stocks, which is coincidental with market events and announcements such as merger activity or new product announcements
- Investment in stocks and companies that are outside the usual scope of a trader's portfolio or focus area
- Unusual level of focus or concentration in one stock
- An investment thesis that is not based on solid research

There are many software tools now available that can apply automated rules-based detection engines that can identify anomalous activity. Use cases can be established leveraging prior examples of insider trading and the types of communication and trading patterns to detect wrongdoing. Investment banks and their trading operations in 2016 will generally use multiple models to detect potential insider trading, front running, collusion, and the like. Since the FX trading scandal, tools and models have also been put in place to surveille trading in those products, where before they were seen as benign areas of activity. These models and tools are audited and tested on a regular basis by the SEC, the OCC, and other regulators. Whether or not these methods are as effective as they might be is an open question that we will come back to. What is not up for debate, however, is the necessity of these checks and balances.

The experience of another ex-colleague serves to illustrate the importance of sharing trading information more openly with the back and middle office team. Mark had been the CFO of several hedge funds and is one of the most experienced on Wall Street. Mark didn't worry too much about appearances. He did not bother to comb his hair or clean his thick glasses. But he was brilliant and he could do his job blind folded. Despite this brilliance, he has twice found himself on the receiving end of portfolio managers who did not provide sufficient transparency into the investment process. The first time, as CFO of a credit fund, he did not have full transparency into the extent of subprime investments in the portfolio. The fund's value was subsequently totally wiped out during the 2008 Financial Crisis. The second time, as CFO of an equities fund, he was not provided with information regarding the nature of the data upon which investments and trades were being made, some of which was later alleged (with ultimately a guilty conviction for several of the portfolio team) by federal prosecutors to be based on inside information. As CFO, Mark was blindsided in both cases, in part because he was, in effect, treated not as an investment partner but as back office. Had he been fully brought into the investment process, with much greater transparency, he may have been able to help avert the crises that overtook the funds in both cases.

Portfolio managers require supervision but very rarely do they ask for it, get it, and accept it. The example of Mark illustrates that there is a heavy unseen cost to insider trading, which is often borne, when firms close, by the hard-working employees in support functions. They, in addition, have not been able to reap the rewards harvested by those responsible for the issues at hand. Ultimately, it becomes harder to attract and retain talent into infrastructure roles in hedge funds and banks when the risks are seen as being too great and the rewards too little relative to the front office. It appears that the low-cost infrastructure, ethical shortfalls, and structural inadequacies of hedge funds are amongst the most pressing issues to address.

Notes

1. A full reading of the Act and its provisions can be found at the following link: https://www.sec.gov/about/laws/sea34.pdf.

2. The Securities Exchange Act of 1934 firmly established the rules against insider trading. The Final Rules established by the Securities and Exchange Commission addressed three issues: the selective disclosure by issuers of material nonpublic information (MNPI); when insider trading liability arises in connection with a trader's "use" or "knowing possession" of MNPI; and when the breach of a family or other nonbusiness relationship may give rise to liability under the misappropriation theory of insider trading. The rules were designed to promote the full and fair disclosure of information by issuers, and to clarify and enhance existing prohibitions against insider trading.

3. Details of the Gupta case were widely reported. A good summary of the issues can be found at Peter Lattman and Azam Ahmed, "Rajat Gupta Convicted of Insider Trading," Dealbook, *The New York Times* (June 15, 2012), https://dealbook.nytimes .com/2012/06/15/rajat-gupta-convicted-of-insider-trading/.

4. Recent court cases in insider trading include: The *Second Circuit in United States v. Newman* in December 2014 and the Supreme Court in *United States v. Salman* in December 2016. The latter upheld a conviction for trading on inside information, arguing that the tipper need not receive a tangible or material benefit from his tips, saying that giving inside information to "a relative or friend" is in itself enough of a

quid-pro-quo personal benefit. It's "the same thing as trading by the tipper followed by a gift of the proceeds," the Court wrote in its opinion. Salman's conduct, the Court added, "is in the heartland" of rules that define insider trading.

5. Several hedge funds closed following insider trading scandals:

   ■ The Galleon Group was one of the largest hedge fund management firms in the world, managing over $7 billion before closing in October 2009 following an insider trading scandal. The firm was founded by Raj Rajaratnam, a former equity research analyst and eventual president of Needham & Company, in 1997.

   ■ Diamondback Capital Management LLC was among the hedge funds raided by the FBI in 2010 in its investigation of insider trading. The company was liquidated after an exodus of clients in December 2012 led to a redemption of over $500 million at the end of 2012. Diamondback had over 130 employees and $6 billion in assets in 2010.

   ■ Frontpoint Partners, once a multi-billion-dollar fund, closed down following an insider trading scandal in 2011 involving an analyst.

   ■ Newcastle Funds closed down following an insider trading scandal involving the fund's portfolio manager.

   ■ SAC was forced to close for outside funds and redeemed all external investors in 2016 after a series of investigations and enquiries by federal prosecutors. Now operating as a vehicle to manage internal funds only, it has been renamed Point72 Asset Management.

6. Labaton Sucharow LLP's survey, "Wall Street in Crisis: A Perfect Storm Looming," (confidentially) polled financial professionals on corporate ethics, wrongdoing in the workplace, and the role of financial regulators in policing the marketplace. The results suggest that the financial services industry faces a serious and growing ethical crisis.

7. A criminal complaint filed in the Federal District Court in Brooklyn in 2016 accused Mark Johnson, the global head of HSBC's foreign exchange cash trading desk, and Stuart Scott, the former head of the bank's currency trading desk for Europe, the Middle East, and Africa, of conspiracy to defraud a company, subsequently identified as Cairn Energy, in a $3.5 billion currency exchange in December 2011. Trial is set for the fall of 2017. See Stewart Bishop, "Trial Set for HSBC Exec Accused of Scamming Forex Trade," Law 360 (November 22, 2016), https://www.law360.com/articles/865599/trial-set-for-hsbc-exec-accused-of-scamming-forex-trade.

CHAPTER 5

Price Manipulation Risk: The Big Unknown

The risk of price manipulation of securities is likely the top banking risk that is least understood by the layman. Indeed, at first blush, the sin of deliberately mispricing a security does not appear the most egregious of financial sins. Yet, as we have seen with the LIBOR scandal, it can lead to significant market distortions, price cheating, and significant penalties from regulators. Understanding the reason why that is so and what can be done to mitigate the risk is one of the most urgent issues for risk managers on Wall Street today.

What catches the headlines is generally the bad actions of a few. However, there are many, many people involved in complex, difficult valuation work that do the right thing every day. Someone wandering through a typical fund accounting operation, for instance, would perhaps be struck by the level of focus and intense effort expended on the activity. Controllers spend a great deal of the day pouring over the valuation of securities in each portfolio. However, any security ultimately depends on there being a market to purchase it. What happens when no one wants to buy the security in question? A precipitous drop in prices can occur. This is what happened to credit securities and subprime securities in the summer of 2007.[1]

Many traders and many firms at that time were depending on the buoyant market in mortgage securities to drive profits and revenue. Instead, these prices suddenly dropped due to change in housing market and associated investment products, and the drop in prices affected the salaries of many. In a market for equities that has typical levels of transparency, the price cannot be hidden or run away from—it is what it is. In the case of mortgage-based credit funds, however, prices depend on the quotes received from the brokers who deal in these securities. These brokers are able to provide prices because they are active in buying and selling these types of securities. When prices started to drop early in the second quarter of 2007, there was much disbelief and skepticism. In a very short time, however, based on the quotes coming back from the brokers, certain securities lost almost all of their value. As funds and banks completed the painstakingly difficult and concentrated work to finalize the impact of the price changes, the loss of values, for the vast majority who held long positions, was an extremely difficult message to publish and not an easy position to be in. In just one example, the valuation of the Bear Stearns High Grade Structured Credit Fund was destroyed almost overnight.[2] The difficulty in communicating what had happened to management, to investors, to the outside world was immense. Not just because the results were so unpalatable for investors but also because they were met by a world with no understanding of the cause. While investors, everyone, can hear every day, every minute, of the gyrations of the stock market, there is no such way for them to gauge or understand the valuations prevailing in the market for certain complex or exotic securities. That is still the case, and that is part of why this risk is still significant for Wall Street. In a world where certain types of securities do not have an easily agreed upon value, there is temptation to manipulate valuations.

Price Manipulation

There are instances where traders are willing and able, on occasion, to manipulate the price of a traded security. Such instances are able to happen when securities are complex, hard to value, and are not traded on a public exchange. In general, of course, trading in marketable securities happens when people can agree on a price to execute a transaction. Most of the time, that price is broadly determined by an exchange and can be tested by analysts and traders on the basis of easily observable data in the market. Transparency is thus facilitated by an exchange and pricing data available to all market participants. Certain securities, however, are valued on the basis of price information that is not so transparent to others. Pricing may, in fact, be dependent on expertise or market data available to a restricted number of persons. Transactions in such securities may also occur not on an exchange but on the basis of a bilateral agreement between two parties. Exotic securities such as structured notes, collateralized debt obligations (CDOs), and credit default swaps (CDS) have been typical of such transactions up to now (though this is now changing for some type of swaps, thanks to the Dodd-Frank legislation). Banks also provide valuation expertise and pricing information that becomes an input into the valuation of securities and assets.

The interest rates at which banks lend to one another and use as benchmarks for other transactions are an example of such valuation services. LIBOR (London Inter-Bank Offered Rate) is the most well-known of these, but there are many others.

It turns out that banks run several risks in this area. First, in the case of transactions in securities that are hard to value, banks run a risk that is hard to measure when they lack an independent and authoritative valuation source for a given security. (Of course, this also has another side to it—an opportunity to realize excess profits.) In such rare cases, traders may be able to, if they are tempted by opportunities to improve their earnings for the year, manipulate the price of the security they hold in their favor. Second, in the case of valuation services, banks are at risk of introducing distortions into the marketplace if they fail to provide objective valuation data. Let's look at three major examples of the several past years.

Earnings Restatements

In early 2008, Credit Suisse restated its earnings from Q3 2007 because of an apparent miscalculation. Restatements like this occur rarely, and it happened in this case in large part due to the deliberately inaccurate valuation of a credit derivative portfolio. Three traders, Salmaan Siddiqui, David Higgs, and Kareem Serageldin, later pled guilty in a Manhattan courtroom to charges of deliberately marking their credit derivatives portfolio at inflated prices to hide hundreds of millions of dollars in losses.[3] How could something like this happen?

Owing to the lack of publicly available pricing data, and in common with general market practice, the Credit Suisse credit portfolio was valued based on the traders obtaining bid and offer quotes from other dealers in the market. In reality, however, according to the criminal complaint, the traders themselves priced the portfolio and the quotes they were using were prices from earlier in 2007, before the beginning of the housing market collapse. The difference in the valuation of the securities once more appropriate quotes were applied was $1.3 billion. In other words, something like a market crash had taken place since the prior quarter, but the portfolio was being valued by these traders as if the market was still buoyant. That way their positions looked good. The interesting thing, and also rather worrying, is that apparently none of the people mandated to provide oversight of the valuation process—in particular, financial controllers, risk managers, and trading supervisors—knew enough to question the values those traders had assigned to the portfolio, as those values were accepted as part of the original financial books for the quarter.

LIBOR

Several banks were in the headlines in 2012 for indiscretions in the setting of interest rates, most notably the LIBOR rate.[4] The charge was that these banks formally admitted that "the manipulation of the (rate) submissions affected the fixed rates on some occasions." The benefit to these banks was, first, to make their businesses appear stronger than they actually were. A lower interest rate implies a perception on the part of the counterparty of a stronger balance sheet, helping to prop up the bank in question through the financial crisis. The second motivation was to trade on small differences in interest rates based on the certain knowledge of what interest rates would be.

Foreign Exchange

In 2015, it was announced that six global banks were to pay more than $5.6 billion to settle allegations that they rigged foreign exchange markets, in a scandal the FBI said involved criminality "on a massive scale."[5] Announcing the settlement, the US Department of Justice said that between December 2007 and January 2013, traders at Citigroup, JPMorgan Chase, Barclays, and the Royal Bank of Scotland, who described themselves as "The Cartel," used an exclusive chat room and coded language to manipulate benchmark exchange rates "in an effort to increase their profits." By agreeing to place orders at a certain time or sharing confidential information, it was possible to move prices more sharply versus working alone where the impact would be smaller. Such price changes close to the time of the pegging of the rate daily could result in advantageous positions, for example, versus client orders currently being worked by traders. That could result in traders making more profits and clients being hurt (see Table 5-1).

Collusion

What all of these cases have in common is a pricing mechanism that is vulnerable to exploitation by manual intervention and collusion between those with a self-interest in doing so. Collusion was active during the FX incident, with

Table 5-1 Losses from Price Manipulation

Firm	Year(s)	Loss (in US billions)	Type	Securities
Multiple	2007–2015	10+	Fines	Forex
Multiple	2007–2016	6+	Fines	LIBOR
CSFB	2008	1.3~	Revised loss amount	Credit securities

traders speaking to each other on the phone or on Internet chat rooms. It can also be implicit, where traders don't need to speak to each other but are still aware of what other people in the market are planning to do. The revelation that traders colluded to move around currency exchange rates was particularly embarrassing for the banks because it occurred after they had paid billions of dollars to settle claims that their traders had tried to rig interbank lending rates. It also raised questions as to whether the industry learned any lessons from the LIBOR or the credit securities scandals.

Some of the key risk indicators and controls included in Figure 5-1 include the following:

■ Traders are able to use two different systems to trade fixed-income securities, allowing them to arbitrage executions between the two.
■ Traders price their securities using nonapproved pricing models.
■ Security price levels do not change even though markets have.
■ Unusual trading activity occurs just before price fixing (usually at market close).
■ Trader has access to control and edit price models.

Although there are many risk indicators, the issue continues to be the opportunity for deliberate price manipulation owing to the obscurity of the valuation drivers. Many of the incidents that have been subject to recent settlements between banks and regulators date back to 2008 or even earlier. Controls have been strengthened since that time, in part due to pressure from regulators to make such improvements. Key controls in Model Risk and Control center on price models and independent price verification. Banks employ large teams of administrators responsible for ensuring that each position on the books is associated with a certified valuation model

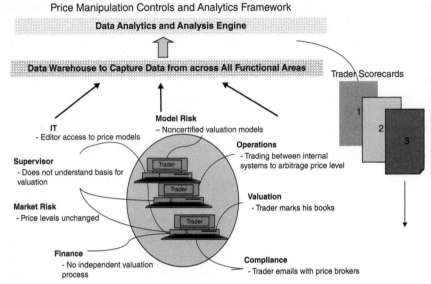

Figure 5-1: Areas of focus to identify risk of price manipulation

and authoritative data source. In addition, price testing is generally conducted on each position on a monthly or quarterly basis by an independent valuation unit.

Emphasis on Surveillance

Banks have long had trade surveillance teams in place to cover the equity trading markets, with the primary objective of uncovering evidence of market manipulation through insider trading, front running, and so on. The lesson learned from the FX and LIBOR scandals is that, first, the FX and LIBOR markets can be manipulated, and second, surveillance is required both of traders and their communications in these markets. Indeed, since these scandals took place, regulators have been requiring via *consent orders* that banks extend and modernize their trade surveillance capabilities to these additional markets. We will discuss in Chapter 21 the opportunities provided by modern computing tools and techniques, particularly in the AI and cognitive space, to strengthen surveillance capabilities.

Despite efforts to strengthen controls, the increased rigor of Model Risk Control being a central element, banks still have exposure to price manipulation risk owing to continuing reliance on manual processes and human intervention for certain hard-to-value securities. Risk managers, therefore, need to continue to focus on improving controls in this space, in particular, to ensure that independent valuation control groups are able to attract high-caliber valuation experts, that traders are not able to manage the pricing process directly, that valuation models are certified and consistently followed, and that manual processes are kept to a minimum.

In the future, the exposure that banks have to this risk should be reduced by the drive toward a more transparent marketplace. We look at this in more detail in Chapter 17.

Notes

1. Reduction in value of credit and mortgage securities that started in the summer of 2007 was driven by the subprime mortgage market. Between 2004 and 2006, the share of subprime mortgages relative to total originations ranged from 18 to 21 percent, versus less than 10 percent between 2001 and 2003 and during 2007. Useful source for the mortgage securities market is the University of North Carolina, Department of Statistics: www.stat.unc.edu/faculty/cji/fys/2012/Subprime% 20mortgage%20crisis.pdf.

2. On June 22, 2007, Bear Stearns pledged a collateralized loan of up to $3.2 billion to "bail out" one of its funds, the Bear Stearns High-Grade Structured Credit Fund, while negotiating with other banks to loan money against collateral to another fund, the Bear Stearns High-Grade Structured Credit Enhanced Leveraged Fund. During the week of July 16, 2007, Bear Stearns disclosed that the two subprime hedge funds had lost nearly all of their value amid a rapid decline in the market for subprime mortgages. Ample coverage of this story can be found at the Wall Street Journal and New York Times web sites.

3. Credit Suisse took a $2.6 billion write-down in March 2008, of which $540 million was linked to the price manipulation activities of several traders. The bank discovered the mispricing in early 2008 and reported it to US and UK authorities. Prosecutors subsequently successfully prosecuted traders for manipulating prices of mortgage securities to give the false impression that their trading books were profitable. Full details can be found at the following link: https://www.justice.gov/ usao-sdny/pr/former-credit-suisse-managing-director-pleads-guilty-connection-scheme-hide-losses

4. The LIBOR scandal was a series of fraudulent actions connected to the LIBOR (London Interbank Offered Rate) and also the resulting investigation and reaction. The LIBOR is an average interest rate calculated through submissions of interest

rates by major banks in London. The scandal arose when it was discovered that banks were falsely inflating or deflating their rates so as to profit from trades, or to give the impression that they were more creditworthy than they were. A number of banks were involved in settlements with US and UK regulators and Justice departments, including Barclays, UBS, Deutsche Bank, and the Royal Bank of Scotland. A good overview of the details of the scandal can be found at New York Times Dealbook at http://www.nytimes.com/interactive/2012/07/10/business/dealbook/behind-the-libor-scandal.html.

5. The Foreign Exchange Scandal followed closely the LIBOR scandal with the revelation that traders were colluding to manipulate currency exchange rates. It raised questions as to whether the industry learned any lessons from the previous scandal. A number of banks settled with US and UK regulators, including JPMorgan, Citigroup, Barclays, Royal Bank of Scotland, Deutsche Bank, and Bank of America. A good overview of the FX scandal can be found at: https://www.nytimes.com/2015/05/21/business/dealbook/5-big-banks-to-pay-billions-and-plead-guilty-in-currency-and-interest-rate-cases.html.

CHAPTER 6

The Mortgage Mess

In January 2013, the US Justice Department slapped Standard & Poor's with a civil law suit for fraud,[1] accusing the credit rating agency of inflating the ratings of securitized mortgage products in the years leading up to the 2008 Financial Crisis. However, the beginnings of the mortgage mess trace back to 2006 and 2007 and some of the key risk indicators that, in retrospect, should have been cause for greater circumspection on the part of some risk managers.

Much of the criticism aimed at Wall Street at the time of the financial crisis and since has been related to its role in the mortgage industry. Creating and trading in securities consisting of groups of mortgages had become a major profit center for banks. It was in no small part the critique of this particular activity that led to the Volcker rule and the proposal to ban proprietary trading for investment banks.

Mortgage Securitization

The key to the mortgage growth or securitization lay in the fact that the greatest risk for a bank is the credit risk it takes on when it executes its basic function—lending money to clients. The implosion of the savings and loans industry was largely due to the large number of loan defaults in the 1980s. After this, broadly speaking, there was no longer the same readiness amongst financial institutions to take over the singular risk of lending money to individuals for the means of purchasing a house. Securitization, then, became a primary means by which the housing market was resurrected in the United States.[2]

Mortgage securitization puts a group of mortgages into a single asset and thereby allows banks to pass on the risks of default to a far wider circle of risk takers. Investors who buy the asset are buying the right to receive a set of cash flows—the mortgage payments—from the underlying mortgages. Should one of those mortgages default or refinance, the risk is ideally sufficiently diversified by the other mortgages to ensure the impact is minimized.

As securitization and financial engineering grew more sophisticated, bundles of mortgages were put together into CDOs (collateralized debt obligations), and this allowed investors flexibility to choose the level of risk they took on. These are called *strips*. Investing in the strips with higher risk profiles within the asset—that is, homebuyers assessed as having a higher likelihood of default—is rewarded with higher yields. This spread of the risk made financial and economic sense and enabled expansion of the home ownership market in the United States.[3]

Unfortunately, other less-attractive features of the market were part and parcel of these developments. First, the complexity of some of the assets made it hard to attach fair value to them, creating potential for the type of mispricing discussed in Chapter 4. These issues were never properly addressed. Second, the split between the banks trading in the assets and the originators of the mortgages meant that the underwriting standards maintained by the originators were not necessarily transparent to those trading in the assets. Furthermore, underwriting standards deteriorated as certain mortgage companies sought an ever-larger slice of the pie. It is fair to say that the securitization process at some point failed investors, as it could be seen as allowing certain firms to write poor-quality loans. Firms were able to increase production by extending loans to people who had no practical ability to repay them. The originators were able to quickly move the poor assets off their balance sheets through the sale of the pools of the loans they had amassed to their investors. While 4 percent of prime fixed-rate securitized mortgage loans in the triple-A universe issued in 2004 were judged in 2010 to be below investment grade, 90 percent of those in 2006 and 2007 were.[4] These flaws in the securitization process, unproblematic at first, led to a negative circle of activity fueled by players who only knew a rising housing market. A rising tide raises all boats, but when the tide goes out, all boats get stuck in the sand. There were indicators that the market for mortgage-based securities was headed south by 2006, but they were largely ignored.

Indicators of Risk

Some people were paying attention to the warning signs in 2006, and even earlier, and acted accordingly. Others were either paying attention but did not feel compelled or able to act or simply didn't notice the risks growing around them. This is a story of these different risk managers: the good, the bad, and the ugly.

The first indicator of risk back in 2006 was a decrease in asset quality. (Figure 6-1 provides a generalized framework for risk indicators.) As has been well documented, the mortgage sales industry expanded tremendously through the early part of the 2000s. To maintain production levels and continue to expand the consumer market, the origination of risky mortgage products with adjustable rates in the "subprime space" became far more widespread: Commentators have estimated that the proportion of subprime mortgages grew from 8 percent in 2004 to about 20 percent in 2006.[5] This trend negatively impacted the underlying quality of the assets being packaged. Investment banks repackaged them into securitized products in 2006 and 2007, making their future cash flows far more vulnerable to changes in underlying market conditions. Risk managers worth their salt took note of the changes in underlying assets and took steps accordingly. Goldman Sachs took aggressive steps, prudently as it turned out, to hedge its positions with regard to the housing market in 2006 and came out as well as any of the major trading houses from the crisis. Many risk managers, however, did not take such steps and, in fact, continued to look for ways to double down on their long positions. Citigroup CEO Charles O. Prince, interviewed by the *Financial Times* in July 2007, said, "As long as the music is playing, you've got to get up and dance," before adding the punch line, "We're still dancing."[6]

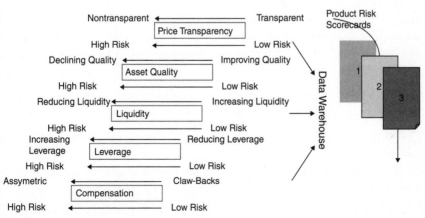

Figure 6-1: Indicators of product risk

The second indicator of risk was a lack of transparency in pricing. These bonds were very complex and the detail behind their underlying assets hard to value. The rating agencies were able to confer value in the marketplace by the ratings they determined. The action just taken by the Department of Justice against S&P underlines the difficulty facing banks. In this context it was important for banks to develop independent means of assessing the value of these securities and of their future prospects. There were several traders who understood that the ratings did not necessarily coincide with market realities—Steve Eisman, Gregory Lippman,[7] and John Paulson,[8] to name just three. Such traders had developed an independent basis for their assessments of value. It is worth noting that when the market was positive, such lack of transparency helped assets of lower quality to attain higher values. When it turned negative, however, that very lack of transparency did not help products that were higher quality: All tended to be tarred with the same brush. Portfolio managers and traders who did detailed analysis of the assets and believed they had a quality portfolio were not necessarily helped if they missed that bigger picture.

The third indicator was a move toward increased leverage that was taking place. It is well known, for example, that leverage levels at Lehman Brothers and Bear Stearns were at historically high levels at the time of their demise in 2008. Hedge funds also looked to increase leverage to increase yield to investors. For example, Bear Stearns launched an "enhanced leverage" version of its High Grade Credit hedge fund in September 2006. While the move toward enhanced leverage was encouraged by investors who were looking to enhance their returns, it was also an indicator of rising risk.

The fourth risk indicator was reducing market liquidity. When liquidity starts to leave the market, risk increases exponentially for those who hold significant long positions. That is why metrics around liquidity are vital to track. Between 2008 and 2011, liquidity literally left the building and those banks, asset managers, and investors holding any type of mortgage security could do nothing with them except count their losses each month. Monitoring for, and being sensitive to, real-time small changes in liquidity levels that suggest larger potential changes could be on their way is extremely useful.[9]

The fifth and final indicator is asymmetric compensation structures: traders paid well for good results without any negative consequences for poor results or negative behaviors. In 2008, the term *clawback* had barely been coined, and clawing back of traders' profits was a reasonably rare event, so this was at best a blunt tool at that time. The increased use of clawbacks has been an encouraging development since that time, though a certain level of clarification and consistency regarding their application would be beneficial. Banks that are more consistent with clear guidelines for their application should be better positioned to manage this type of risk.

At a certain point, the securitized mortgage market turned in a most decisive way but nobody could tell you exactly when that tipping point was reached. As the changes in the mortgage market coursed their way to the trading floors of investment banks and hedge funds, Goldman's risk managers were watching and took actions accordingly when their indicators pointed to changes in market conditions. Others who failed to do so were left holding the bag. This survey of risk indicators, which is hardly exhaustive, does nonetheless highlight the importance of clawbacks and the need for risk managers to understand and track risk indicators from each of the major risk disciplines: market, credit, and operational.

The Aftermath

Not only did Wall Street firms suffer losses in the market from securities they held, they also suffered losses because they invested in companies that originated mortgages and then sold them to those that securitized the loans. Bank of America was the most notable to do this, with its ill-fated purchase of Countrywide Financial, but other banks that made purchases, sometimes at the behest of regulators in the case of JPMorgan and Bear Stearns, suffered a similar fate.[10] In the end, not only did Bank of America and others have to write down the value of such operations and many of the loans that they had written, they also inherited regulatory issues that culminated in fines or a requirement to compensate Fannie Mae or other agencies for loans that were not what they purported to be in terms of underlying loans riskiness. Additionally, the increase in loan default led, in turn, to a rush to foreclose and a further round of regulatory actions, some of the most sizable in history. This is one strong argument for a more deliberate and risk-based strategic planning process on the part of banks. Seven years later, the price of failing to do so came due.

What the story illustrates is not the wickedness of Wall Street but the level of complexity that was created. An on button had been pressed, but there was no off switch or set of brakes that could be applied. In the end, the momentum generated by the securitization industry was too great to stop. There could only be one ending to this trip.

In addition to the individual improvements that firms can make to their risk management processes, making sure that there are brakes that can be applied when the market overheats is of critical importance. The way this works in most markets is through the organization of a marketplace, which provides clearer indicators of its direction, levels of supply and demand, and pricing to participants. The moves made in the past several years toward a central, transparent marketplace for fixed-income securities should support this development.

However, risk managers must still be vigilant to markets exhibiting the type of characteristics of the mortgage underwriting market that we reviewed earlier in the chapter. Cognitive tools and technologies can be applied to automate the detection of such concerning market features as reducing asset quality, shorter product approval timelines, and evidence of waivers of the usual credit score features in, for example, communication between customers. The use of such tools, in combination with the judgment of the risk manager, will support reducing the likelihood of such future disasters on both the micro and macro level.

Notes

1. The rating agencies played and continue to play a major role in the mortgage market by providing a rating opinion of the creditworthiness of the bonds that are issued backed by mortgage loans: mortgage-backed securities (MBS), CDOs, and so on. Following the financial crisis, many buyers of the securities in question alleged that rating agencies failed to do due diligence on many of the bonds they rated. This was particularly in respect of CDOs that were later identified as subprime loans and highly exposed to potential default. After many calls for an investigation, the US Department of Justice charged S&P with a deliberate attempt to inflate the ratings of bonds it rated.

2. In 1981, Fannie Mae issued its first mortgage pass-through, called a *mortgage-backed security*. In 1983, Freddie Mac issued the first collateralized mortgage obligation. From there growth was rapid. In 2001, $1.09 trillion of MBS were issued in the United States, and in 2003, $2 trillion were issued.

3. Home ownership rate in the United States is measured by the Vacancy Rate survey conducted annually by the US Census Bureau. According to this survey, the home ownership rate was stable at around 64 percent from 1970 to 1994. The next decade, however, saw an increase in the home ownership rate to 69 percent, where

the rate remained until 2006. Then the rate declined as the economy did with the outset of the financial crisis to 67.4 percent in 2009.

4. Laurie Goodman, "Securitization Panel," Amherst Securities Group LP (July 15, 2010), http://www.sifma.org/events/2010/647/pdf/sifma-summit-07152010.pdf.

5. Michael Simkovic, "Competition and Crisis in Mortgage Securitization," *Indiana Law Journal* 88, no. 1 (Winter 2013), http://www.repository.law.indiana.edu/cgi/viewcontent.cgi?article=11040&context=ilj.

6. Citigroup CEO Charles O. Prince was interviewed by the *Financial Times* in July 2007. This quote made the headlines at the time, and it was not long after that Prince left Citi following a poor quarter in November 2007 as a result of CDO- and MBS-related losses.

7. Michael Lewis, *The Big Short: Inside the Doomsday Machine* (New York: W. W. Norton & Company, 2010). Lewis describes several of the key players in the creation of the credit default swap market that sought to bet against the collateralized debt obligation (CDO) bubble and thus ended up profiting from the financial crisis of 2007–2010. His book also highlights the eccentric nature of the type of person who bets against the market or goes against the grain. Two of the managers featured include Steve Eisman, an outspoken hedge fund manager, and Greg Lippmann, a Deutsche Bank trader.

8. Gregory Zuckerman, *The Greatest Trade Ever: The Behind-the-Scenes Story of How John Paulson Defied Wall Street and Made Financial History* (New York: Crown Business, 2010). The scale of Paulson's big bet, "the greatest trade ever" as Greg Zuckerman describes it, was extraordinary. By piling into complex credit default swaps against mortgages—in effect, insurance policies that would pay out if homeowners defaulted—his fund made an unthinkable $15 billion (£9.8 billion) in a year, $4 billion of which he took home himself.

9. For a scholarly article on the financial crisis and liquidity, you could do worse than read M. K. Brunmeier, "Deciphering the Liquidity and Credit Crunch 2007–2008," *Journal of Economic Perspectives* 23, no. 1 (Winter 2009), pp. 77–100.

10. Acquisitions:
    - On July 1, 2008, Bank of America Corporation completed its purchase of Countrywide Financial Corporation. The costs of the purchase amounted to as much as $40 billion according to some estimates, taking into account loans that went sour and penalty payments required by regulators and the like.
    - The purchase of Bear Stearns at $10 per share cost JPMorgan Chase an initial $1.5 billion. Subsequent settlements with regulators and investors may have added as much as $13 billion to the bill. However, JPMorgan's investment banking revenues have also increased since the purchase.

■ On Sunday, September 14, 2008, Bank of America announced it was in talks to purchase Merrill Lynch for $38.25 billion in stock. *The Wall Street Journal* reported later that day that Merrill Lynch was sold to Bank of America for 0.8595 shares of Bank of America common stock for each Merrill Lynch common share, or about $50 billion or $29 per share. Regulatory fines and lawsuits paid by Bank of America following the purchase have further added to the bill.

CHAPTER 7

Ponzi Schemes and Snake Oil Salesmen

This chapter is concerned with financial institutions that use illegal methods to gain investors and buyers. The first section deals with investment managers who do this by falsely pumping up their performance in the manner of Ponzi schemes ala Madoff. The second section deals with financial institutional salespeople who smooth-talk and graft their way into the graces of individuals, pension funds, institutional clients, banks, charities and trusts through the old-fashioned methods known as bribery and corruption. Finally, we will then look at how these tried and trusted methods for fooling people and for taking advantage of fools can be countered.

Ponzi Schemes

Much has been written and said about Bernie Madoff, but he was neither the first nor the last to conjure a money-making machine out of thin air.

In 1920 in Boston, Charles Ponzi's supposed arbitrage scheme was just a masquerade for paying off early investors with the deposits of later investors. Ponzi claimed he would double investors' money in 90 days through a bizarre plan to buy and resell international postal-reply coupons. Ponzi collected more than $8 million from about 30,000 investors in just seven months before the scheme collapsed. He served five years in prison for using the mail to defraud. Thus, the Ponzi scheme was born. A bit later, Swedish businessman Ivar Kreuger, known as the *match king,* built his own Ponzi scheme, defrauding investors based on the supposedly fantastic profitability and ever-expanding nature of his match monopolies. The scheme collapsed in the 1930s, and Kreuger shot himself.

Bernie Madoff, however, was responsible for the most significant Ponzi scheme in history. On December 10, 2008, Madoff made an admission to his sons that his investments were "all one big lie." The following day, he was arrested and charged with a single count of securities fraud. At the time of his arrest, the losses were estimated to be $65 billion, making it the largest investor fraud in history. It is probably fair to say that calculations have still not arrived at an accurate estimate of investors' loss, but it is fair to say that they were in multiple billions of dollars. Madoff was sentenced to 150 years in prison.

Much has been written about Madoff, including several books about the scheme, how it was able to continue for so long, and how he was able to keep the scheme a secret from even those closest to him. One of the interesting things about Madoff, of course, is that he was able to fool seemingly very smart people, including the most sophisticated of investors. Madoff founded the Wall Street firm Bernard L. Madoff Investment Securities LLC in 1960, and was its chairman until his arrest. He was active in the National Association of Securities Dealers (NASD), a self-regulatory securities industry organization, serving as the chairman of the board of directors and on the board of governors. In 1992, *The Wall Street Journal* described him as "one of the masters of the off-exchange 'third market' and the bane of the New York Stock Exchange. He has built a highly profitable securities firm, Bernard L. Madoff Investment Securities."

This operation was, of course, very helpful in burnishing Madoff's reputation on Wall Street as he started to build out the fund side of the business in the 1980s. He gave interviews to the press and was able to talk intelligently about his esoteric hedging strategy. However, a few analysts performing due diligence had been unable to replicate the Madoff fund's past returns using historic price data for US stocks and options on the indexes, his claimed strategy. *Barron's* raised the possibility that Madoff's returns were most likely due to front running his firm's brokerage clients.

Mitchell Zuckoff, professor of journalism at Boston University and author of *Ponzi's Scheme: The True Story of a Financial Legend,* says that "the 5% payout rule," a federal law requiring private foundations to pay out 5 percent of their funds each year, allowed Madoff's Ponzi scheme to go undetected for a long period since he managed money mainly for charities. Zuckoff noted, "For every $1 billion in foundation investment, Madoff was effectively on the hook for about $50 million in withdrawals a year. If he was not making real investments, at that rate the principal would last 20 years. By targeting charities, Madoff could avoid the threat of sudden or unexpected withdrawals."

In his guilty plea, Madoff admitted that he hadn't actually traded since the early 1990s, and all of his returns since then had been fabricated.

Madoff, of course, invested in the sort of outward signs of success and swagger that likely filled those around him, including clients, with confidence. Madoff maintained sole ownership of the company throughout its history and retained close control over back-office oversight functions. He was thus able to ensure that only he knew about the various steps in his fictitious scheme, such as maintenance of a fictitious banks address to which all bank document requests were sent and intercepted (by him), as well as falsification of bank statements and confirmations.

One can easily understand why Madoff's investors were misled. Its reputation as a hard-to-get-into fund provided allure. The support of trading experts burnished Madoff's reputation. The implication of an edge provided by the securities operation was perhaps the most persuasive reason why Madoff was seen as such a solid bet. Indeed, The SEC investigated Madoff in 1999 and 2000 about concerns that the firm was hiding its customers' orders from other traders, for which Madoff then took corrective measures. In 2001, an SEC official met with Harry Markopolos at its Boston regional office and reviewed his allegations of Madoff's fraudulent practices.[1] The SEC claimed it conducted two other inquiries into Madoff, but did not find any violations or major issues of concern. In 2007, SEC enforcement completed an investigation it had begun on January 6, 2006, into a Ponzi scheme allegation. This investigation resulted in neither a finding of fraud nor a referral to the SEC Commissioners for legal action.

Concerns were also raised that Madoff's auditor of record was Friehling & Horowitz, a two-person accounting firm based in suburban Rockland County that had only one active accountant, David G. Friehling, a close Madoff family friend. Typically, hedge funds hold their portfolio at a securities firm (a major bank or brokerage), which acts as the fund's prime broker. This arrangement allows outside investigators to verify the holdings. Madoff's firm was its own broker-dealer and allegedly processed all of its trades. Ironically, Madoff, a pioneer in electronic trading, refused to provide his clients online access to their accounts. He sent out account statements by mail, unlike most hedge funds, which emailed statements.

Four years after the 2008 discovery of Madoff's scheme there was a similar incident involving Peregrine Financial Group, a firm that operated for over 20 years in relative obscurity in Cedar Falls, Iowa. Peregrine's founder, Russell Wasendorf Sr., following a suicide attempt and business failure, pled guilty and was sentenced to 50 years in prison for four counts of embezzling clients out of more than $100 million, commission of mail fraud, and two counts of lying to federal regulators. This disturbing episode highlighted once again the risk of fraudulent investment schemes paying investors returns from their own money or subsequent investors' money.

Wasendorf's company, known to most of its clients as PFGBest, developed a reputation, just like Madoff's did, in its formative years for pioneering new electronic trading platforms and reliable customer service. One can still find on its website a steady accumulation of top futures broker awards, even through 2012, and a long list of customer testimonials. Wasendorf, like Madoff, became an industry acolyte and was sought out to take on industry guardianship roles. He served most significantly on the National Futures Association (NFA), the self-regulated watchdog of the futures industry, Advisory Committee. He invested in the sort of outward signs of success and swagger that likely filled those around him, including clients, with confidence: a spectacular headquarters, private jets, and so on. Like Madoff, Wasendorf maintained sole ownership of the company throughout its history and retained close control over back-office oversight functions. According to his own admissions, he allowed no one else at the firm to communicate with regulators, auditors, and banks. He was thus able to ensure that only he knew about the various steps in his fictitious scheme, such as maintenance of a fictitious banks address to which all bank document requests were sent and intercepted (by him), as well as falsification of bank statements and confirmations. As with Madoff, the PFGBest's auditor was a one-person shop[2] based at the accountant's home. We have read this story before. Like Madoff, Wasendorf's firm employed a small army of sales people who worked to introduce new accounts and new money to the firm. Also like Madoff, the lies finally caught up with him but only after a very long run.

Stanford Financial Group, was another Ponzi scheme that was identified in the late 2000's. In early 2009, the founder, Allen Stanford, became the subject of several fraud investigations, and on February 17, 2009, was charged by the US Securities and Exchange Commission (SEC) with fraud and multiple violations of US securities laws for alleged "massive ongoing fraud" involving $7 billion in certificates of deposits (https://www.theguardian.com/world/2012/jun/14/allen-stanford-jailed-110-years). Ultimately Stanford was sentenced to 110 years of prison. His exploits were detailed in many newspapers at the time: The UK Guardian newspaper covered his specific methods in some depth in a profile written on February 20, 2009, and the *New Yorker* had a longer profile in March 2009. Like the other Ponzi schemers we have looked at, Stanford was a past master at simulation of high returns, making good use of excellent connections and burnishing the high life he lived, in this case, in the Carribean.

Table 7-1 Losses from Recent Ponzi Schemes

Firm	Year	Loss (in US billions)	Product
Platinum Partners	2016	~$1	Hedge Fund
Peregrine	2012	Unknown	Futures Broker
Stanford	2011	~$8	Bank
Madoff	2009*	~$17	Hedge Fund

*Early estimates of losses of $60 billion to investors were not accurate as they included fictitious gains on original investments. The court appointed trustee estimated actual losses to investors to be closer to $18 billion.

More recently, Platinum Partners has been alleged to be the subject of a similar scandal. In December 2016, federal agents arrested Mark Nordlicht, a founder and the chief investment officer of Platinum, and six others on charges related to a $1 billion fraud that led the firm to be operated "like a Ponzi scheme," prosecutors said (http://www.wsj.com/articles/platinum-partners-executives-charged-with-1-billion-securities-fraud-1482154926). This case shows that, far from going away, the danger posed by Ponzi schemes is ever present. See Table 7-1 for an overview of recent infamous Ponzi schemes.

Regulators and Fraud

At the time the Madoff scheme was revealed in 2008, people found it hard to understand why and how the SEC failed to uncover it earlier and why Madoff was able to get away with it for so long. History is always written, it can't be helped, from the perspective of the outcome. In retrospect, and from the various red flags, it seems obvious that Madoff was a crook. Yet, as one member of the SEC's enforcement team told me, it was virtually impossible to tell: redemptions to investors' requests were always paid out on time; investors' statements looked completely authentic; and there was a separate broker-dealer with its own set of assets that were real. All of this made it extremely difficult to uncover the scheme. After Madoff was charged, as already discussed, some industry analysts said they had reported a concern to the SEC, which the SEC allegedly failed to fully investigate However, relative to the hundreds of investors who had money with Madoff, the number of those who thought something was amiss was very low. Nevertheless, with Madoff and later Wasendoff, there is a set of risk factors or indicators that should be reviewed in conjunction with assessing this risk (see Figure 7-1).

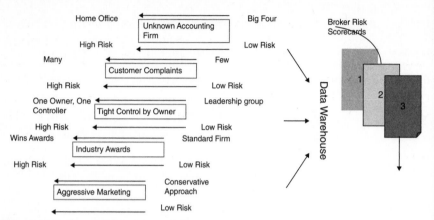

Figure 7-1: Ponzi risk factor analysis

Customers and the CFTC should watch out for an aggressive sales approach, secrecy, and a high-rolling lifestyle, not to mention investor complaints, unknown accountants, and other service providers. But such a set of indicators as these can only be a starting point for deep analysis and can by no means offer sufficient protection on its own. What can the CFTC and other regulators do to prevent such blatant fraud in the future? CFTC Commissioner Scott O'Malia, who chairs the Commission's Technology Advisory Board, was reported at an industry roundtable in 2013 as saying that it will only be through robust surveillance automation and analytics that this problem can ultimately be solved.[3] To this end, he was also reported to say that while progress has been made in IT investments, he still believes much more investment is needed in data mining capabilities. In other words, while the data are there, knowing what to do with them, and specifically how to mine them to identify exceptions and patterns of bad behaviors, is yet to be solved. On this basis, it is clearly too soon to declare victory, but the increasing power of computers and the availability of artificial intelligence data analysis techniques will make this nut easier to crack in the future.

Bribery and Corruption

The temptations of bribery and corruption for some in positions of authority and influence are hard to resist, and for the snake oil salesman can lead to new business just as easily as inflating investment performance.

In the international arena, the Foreign Corrupt Practices Act (FCPA) has long been in place to make it unlawful for US companies and companies issuing stock in the United States to make payments to foreign government officials to assist in obtaining or retaining business. In 2010, the SEC's Enforcement Division created a specialized unit to further enhance its enforcement of the FCPA. A spate of cases has resulted from that across all industries. Cases specific to banks and financial services include one involving a former Morgan Stanley employee in China in 2012, a second involving the hedge fund, Och-Ziff in South Africa in 2016, and a third involving JPMorgan, again in China.[4]

Bribery and corruption is also a way to sell business in the United States. This was illustrated by the pay-to-play scandal, which first embroiled the New York State Retirement Fund in 2010 and resulted, amongst other things, in a guilty plea by former comptroller, Alan Hevesi.[5] This was followed more recently by further allegations of corruption announced by the US attorney for the Southern District of New York in December 2016. The details this time involved Navnoor Kang, fixed-income manager for the Fund. The lurid details include gifts of Rolex watches, free travel, and various other unsolicited benefits made by brokers, Deborah Kelly and Gregg Schonhorn, looking to place business with the Fund. This second incident occurred despite the fact that New York had instituted certain safeguards following the first scandal. CalPERS, the California pension fund, has also suffered from pay-to-play scandals with Fred Buenrostro, the former chief executive, pleading guilty to doing so in 2014.[6]

What can be done to identify such nefarious activities? What concerns us here is not so much the corruption of those in public office but the illegal methods employed by some brokers and institutions to secure business. What should be done to mitigate? First, institutions and their compliance departments need to put in place policies and procedures to guard against such activity. Education is paramount, but clearly this is not enough. Specific compliance functions must be established responsible for identifying and rooting out corrupt practices both at home and abroad. Most international banks have by now established officers and function responsible for identifying foreign corrupt practices, but similarly focused domestic functions also should be established. Second, placement agents that act as middlemen between asset managers and pension funds and the like must be subject to special attention. They are responsible for steering a very significant amount of business to pension funds.[7] Are they really providing a quality service and helping pension funds to make better decisions about the asset managers they are using? Are their activities and recommendations based on legitimate and quantitative analysis? A 2015 study found that private equity funds using placement agents underperformed the market by as much as 3.5 percent annually.[8] In other words, most pension funds appear not to get value from placement agents. The study also found that exclusive relationships between pension funds and placement agents lead to negative outcomes.

Lastly, managers need to be vigilant in monitoring employee activities, sudden changes in lifestyle and unexpected lavishness of dress or behavior, and their communications.

Monitoring employee communications is more important and challenging than ever. With social media, instant messaging, chat rooms, and the like, banks and brokers have multiple channels of communication. How do firms monitor all these channels? Although there are regulatory requirements for firms to monitor and capture all client-facing employee communications, technologies have not been available to do so in a comprehensive way. One trick, for example, that such technologies must master is tracing the different IDs that employees take on across different channels of communication to a single person. For example, an identity on LinkedIn or Facebook needs to be traced back to the official firm email address. Another trick is ingesting all these communications into a single authoritative data source. Just like firms have official financial books and records, so they need official books and records for their electronic communications. It is critical when doing so to maintain the context of those communications and the chain of custody within a given conversation. Once these communications are captured, alerts can be generated for potential policy violations by the use of lexicons and advanced search capabilities to highlight conversations of interest.

Such tools are improving rapidly by arming these tools with greater language capabilities and the ability to distinguish between benign conversations and non-benign. For example, a conversation between two colleagues discussing whether to buy tickets for the Giants game is benign. A conversation discussing whether or not to buy tickets for a client who manages the New York pension fund is not. This is another place where artificial intelligence (AI) and cognitive technologies can provide greater insight because these technologies can learn to set the first one aside to focus on the second. Normal, rule-based software cannot do so. Although the best answer is for public officials to cut out the middleman and do the hard work of choosing the best supplier of financial services for themselves, the reality is that the middleman will continue to ply his trade and attract business in doing so. Mitigating the risk of bribery and corruption by adopting these controls and tools will continue to be required in the future.

Notes

1. There were some who questioned Madoff and his consistent returns:

   - Erin Arvedlund (a financial journalist), "Don't Ask, Don't Tell—Bernie Madoff Is So Secretive, He Even Asks Investors to Keep Mum," *Barron's* (May 7, 2001).

   - Harry Markoplos, a forensic auditor and forensic fraud investigator, analyzed Madoff's performance and concluded it was a Ponzi scheme. He alerted the SEC in 2000, 2001, and 2004 but apparently the SEC did not follow up with a full investigation.

2. Peregrine's long-time auditor Veraja-Snelling ran her tiny accounting firm from a Chicago suburb. In August 2013, Snelling was banned by the Commodity Futures Trading Commission from performing audits for firms it oversees.

3. Timothy Bourgaize Murray, "CFTC's O'Malia Says Tech Training Wheels Are Off," *Waters Technology* (February 2013).

4. The SEC website provides good information on the cases that they have charged and settled:

   - Former Morgan Stanley executive: SEC charged Garth R. Peterson with secretly acquiring millions of dollars worth of real estate investments for himself and an influential Chinese official who in turn steered business to Morgan Stanley's funds. He agreed to a settlement in which he is permanently barred from the securities industry and must pay more than $250,000 in disgorgement and relinquish his approximately $3.4 million interest in Shanghai real estate acquired in his scheme (SEC website, April 25, 2012).

   - Och-Ziff agreed to pay $412 million in civil and criminal matters, and CEO Daniel Och agreed to pay $2.2 million to settle charges against him (SEC website, September 29, 2016).

   - JPMorgan agreed to pay $264 million to the SEC, Justice Department, and Federal Reserve to settle charges that it corruptly influenced government officials and won business in the Asia-Pacific region by giving jobs and internships to their relatives and friends (SEC website, November 17, 2016).

5. On October 7, 2010, Alan Hevesi pleaded guilty to accepting gratuities for steering the investment funds to California venture capitalist Elliot Broidy. Hevesi had accepted $75,000 in trips for himself and his family and $500,000 in campaign contributions, and benefited from $380,000 given to a lobbyist. http://www.nydailynews.com/news/crime/ex-controller-alan-hevesi-actress-peggy-lipton-caught-huge-pension-bribery-scandal-article-1.432050.

6. Fred Buenrostro's "crime was steering more than $3 billion in funds to the private equity firm Apollo Global Management after being bribed by a placement agent firm headed by Alfred Villalobos, the former deputy mayor of Los Angeles. Mr. Buenrostro had received $200,000 in cash placed in shoe boxes." "Former CalPERS Chief Admits Accepting Bribes Stuffed in Paper Bags, Shoe Box in Guilty Plea," CBS Sacramento (July 11, 2014), http://sacramento.cbslocal.com/2014/07/11/former-calpers-chief-admits-accepting-bribes-stuffed-in-paper-bags-shoe-box-in-guilty-plea/.

7. Steven Davidoff Solomon, "After Scandals, Evaluating Pension Funds; Middleman," *New York Times* Dealbook (May 12, 2015). Preqin Private Equity blog, referenced by *New York Times* Dealbook (May 12, 2015), found that, the California Public Employees' Retirement System, the large state pension agency better known as CalPERS, invested in 784 funds using placement agents from 1991 to 2011. That's about 27 percent of the funds CalPERS invested in during that time, making a full-time business for placement agents.

8. Ibid. "A new study—written by Steven Davidoff Solomon, Stephen McKeon of the University of Oregon, and Matthew D. Cain, a financial economist at the S.E.C...examines placement agent investments from 1991 to 2011. That covered 32,526 investments in 4,335 private equity funds." In the 20-year period of the study, only three such funds had an exclusive relationships with a pension fund. All three—Arvco Capital Research, the Wetherly Capital Group and Diamond Edge Capital Partners—had employees convicted in pay-to-play scandals.

CHAPTER 8

Rogue Computer

Faulty software led Knight Capital Group to record thousands of erroneous trades with the NYSE, leading to huge losses and imminent bankruptcy.[1] The Facebook IPO was going to be the IPO to end all IPOs. It all went wrong, however, on the day due to software glitches.[2] The error's ripple effects lasted for days, and some market participants experienced significant losses. Another problematic IPO in 2012, though less high profile, was the BATS (Better Alternative Trading System) public filing, which had to be canceled due to software glitches. These events threw a spotlight on critical execution aspects of technology in facilitating trading activity and potential sources of great operational risk therein.

History of Technology in Public Markets and Increasing Risk

It is doubtful that any CEO of a major brokerage house at the beginning of 2012 would have listed technology failures in sales and trading and IPOs as leading candidates for public relations disasters and major financial losses. Yet in the space of a few short months, the BATS IPO, the Facebook IPO, and Knight Capital all grabbed headlines and losses for the wrong reasons. Given the rapid growth of technology in all aspects of the market, however, such events should not have been a big surprise and while attention is still focused here, it is worthwhile reviewing recent developments and what can be done to address these issues.

The use of technology has been a feature of public stock exchanges since they were first established in Europe over 400 years ago. Such exchanges were enabled by a combination of demand, regulation, and technology. In the twentieth century, telephones and ticker tapes led the way to rapid volume growth.

Modern computer technology was introduced in the 1970s, and its associated efficiencies hastened the onset of much greater trading volumes. All of these developments took place within a market that was dominated by several major players, such as the New York Stock Exchange and the London Stock Exchange, which innovated to stay competitive.

The introduction of screen-based automated quotation systems took place in the mid-1980s. In London, this was known as the Big Bang.[3] This was quickly followed by the stock market crash in 1987, known as Black Monday.[4] This was an early harbinger of the relationship between technical advance, trading volume growth, and more rapid and larger swings in the prices quoted on the trading floor or on the trading screen. Many critics expressed the view that the crash was directly caused by a feedback technology loop that had the effect of compounding price changes. There was some evidence for that view, but since then trading technology has only leapt further ahead, enabling the proliferation of a vast array of new players and new dynamics into the market.

First, electronic markets were one of the key new power groups in the trading marketplace and they reduced the hegemony of the traditional markets and the longstanding nature of their conventions, middlemen, practices, and cost structures.[5] Second, the retail stock trader became a much-noted feature of the market in the wake of these technology developments. The price of placing trades and the easy availability of market information made stock trading a much more attractive proposition to ordinary retail investors. Third, hedge funds with their endless appetite and penchant for secrecy, drove much of the build out of dark pools, so-called because they could conceal the deals coming in to the market as well as superfast trade execution engines.[6] Hedge funds introduced high-frequency trading strategies, and the related algorithmic trading patterns[7] brought back the specter of volume and price dysfunction.

Lastly, technology IPOs, especially the wildly popular ones released on a diversity of new platforms, introduced an element of surprise and excitement into the normally conservative proceedings of the market.

With all this innovation, technology became a major source of risk and potential disruption by the early 2000s. The Flash Crash in May 2010 was a wake-up call to regulators and market participants alike.[8] A rogue algorithmic trade appeared to send US markets sharply down in the space of 20 minutes before rebounding in a similar period. The SEC introduced a number of measures designed to bolster market stability and investor confidence, including a break in the glass utility in cases of precipitous falls in stock value and an improved audit trail of market actions preceding such types of events.

However, like the introduction of safety belts and air bags in cars, these innovations likely only encourage participants to drive faster. Furthermore,

Table 8-1 Losses from IT Failures

Firm	Year	Loss (in US billions)
Knight Capital	2012	~$0.4
NASDAQ	2012	~$0.6
BATS	2012	Unknown
Flash Crash	2010	Unknown

writing rules for every eventuality and identifying every flawed practice in every participant is not possible. The Knight Capital and Facebook cases are only the most well-known and significant in a series of high-frequency market-making, algorithmic trade, and IPO malfunctions that have occurred on different platforms in each region of the globe (see Table 8-1). The challenges and problematic scenarios for regulators and market participants are clearly broader than simply the popular bogeyman—high-speed trading.

Flash Crash 2010

How quickly one executes trades has become a major source of competitive advantage. In equity markets, for many players, it is not what you know but how quickly you can act on it. Nanoseconds matter. By locating servers that route trades ever closer to the market, by building faster computers, market makers can build their market share. Algorithms are deployed that enable market participants to execute trades using preset parameters based on volume levels, price changes, volatility indicators, and so on. Many of these algorithms are similar so that, given certain prevailing market conditions, firms will start to execute in the same direction at the same time. Most of the time, the impacts of such changes are limited since prices go up and down, for the most part, in a continuous way—down like a waterfall and up like an airplane. What happens, however, when price discontinuity is introduced into the market, when a plane plunges from 20,000 feet to a hundred feet? The consequences are generally unknowable because the number of algorithmic traders is huge and knowing how they will react given a certain set of highly unlikely market conditions is impossible.

In May 2010, when a computerized algorithm burst into a selling frenzy, the consequences could probably have been a lot worse. The rogue algorithm set off a tremendous wave of selling activity, and prices of certain securities underwent, in apparent reaction, price drops of very significant proportions. Indeed certain securities, for example, Accenture, went to close to zero value in the space of seconds. Such a drop in value was not related to changes in Accenture's profits or its perceived value. No doubt, Accenture consultants were no more or less busy on this day than any other. In fact, the losses were caused by an automated chain reaction resulting from the unusual levels of activity in apparently unrelated trades.

What the episode showed, like in the market crash as a result of the bursting of the housing bubble, is that in today's market, all markets are interconnected. But maybe it was ever thus, and the innovations brought by technology speed up (in nanoseconds) the falling dominoes before a course correction takes place. In this instance, at least, market losses were minimal, due in no small part to the sensible and prompt actions taken by market regulators. Based on certain criteria, buyers and sellers were put back to the position they were before the crash.

However, people were spooked: investors, regulators, banks, and Washington. The concern was that this was yet another example of a risk, like insider trading, like price manipulation, like rogue trading, that left market participants at the mercy of forces beyond their control. If no rational explanation could be found, the fear of reoccurrence could have a chilling effect on the market. The Senate ordered an investigation, as did the CFTC, SEC, and the Federal Reserve. What was the cause, how could it be fixed?

The Senate Committee that led the investigation concluded that the direct cause of the crash was an algorithm of a futures firm that executed massive sales of index futures.[9] Regardless of the cause, circuit breakers (break-the-glass utilities) were implemented to stop market activity in the instance of certain price changes within a small time period. Every brokerage house was forced to comply.

Other important concerns have emerged since then—namely, that the speed of certain players was such that they were able to gain an unfair market advantage over other market participants.[10] The advantage was measured in pennies, but pennies add up when applied to trades worth millions of dollars. Given both these issues, the SEC conducted examinations of the high-speed trading operations of the large investment banks and broker-dealers. The goal was as much fact-finding as anything else. There had been so much innovation in the market that the SEC was no longer able to monitor market developments. Examiners went in with many questions. For the banks and employees answering them, they were confused: What were the examinations really designed to achieve, what was the focus? Be that as it may, without requiring any significant changes of the front office, IT departments received the brunt of examiners' requests: more rigor when they changed the software code that controlled trading activities, improved security, and regulatory scrutiny over trading algorithms.

So then the same thing couldn't happen again. Right? No, that would be wrong.

Knight Capital 2012

In 2012, Knight Capital made an apparent error in releasing software updates to the live market environment. As a result, Knight Capital was taken on a buying spree of securities it apparently had no wish or had even considered buying. Eventually, the positions added up to a financial obligation that was beyond Knight Capital's financial means. The errant program had, evidently, locked the firm into price points that were above the market price. Unlike the 2010 Flash Crash, exiting the positions in this instance led to real losses and the firm's failure and subsequent sale.

The release of new code into the marketplace is a daily occurrence. While the coding of new software enabling a firm to take advantage of small market movements in new and innovative ways is relatively easy, managing the safe release of such software into the live market environment is hard. This was something, at least, that Knight Capital had failed to do. As it turned out, Knight's very survival depended on its ability to do so. It is doubtful, however, that Knight Capital was fully aware of its top risk or the fact that there was zero tolerance for such a failure.

Facebook and BATS

IPOs also gave rise to such problems in two cases: first, with the Facebook IPO and, second, with the BATS IPO.

The case of Facebook was well reported at the time, of course, and is well-known. NASDAQ failed to execute in a timely way the order flow for the newly issued Facebook stock. Confirmations were not sent out per requirement to communicate to brokers how many shares they had bought. In one instance at UBS, it was reported that brokers, since they did not receive confirmations, placed the order multiple times, leading to a position many times larger than intended and to losses reported in the press to be as high as $400 million. Described to me by a colleague as behavior like a child who keeps pressing a button that doesn't work, this was driven by investors frantic to purchase the stock, and the failure of the market to work properly only exacerbated that. Many other firms and investors were impacted by the failure of the technology to work the way it was supposed to. Of course, the stock price dropped after the failure, and it is likely that the technology failures contributed to this, too.

Diagnosis of the failure was again due to changes introduced into software that were not effectively tested prior to prime time. The BATS IPO in 2012 was a similar failure. In this case, BATS decided to launch its IPO on its own market platform.[11] The failure of the software to handle the IPO was not the best advertisement for the company. Fortunately, the company was able to cancel the IPO without any impacts other than to BATS's own reputation.

How Problems Occur

As a manufacturing process, the development of software is still relatively immature. It is also dynamic and generally part of a larger whole, which has a complex set of links and dependencies. These dependencies need to be carefully documented so that an integration with a new version can ensure that the integrity of those links and dependencies are maintained. When one understands that any single one of the links and interlocking parts may also be changed at any time, one can see how carefully the process of changing, communicating, and testing code needs to be managed.

Careful code release into a live market environment should only happen after the completion of thorough testing to ensure the behavior of software in the live environment has been fully vetted. Such risk management is not necessarily practiced by all players releasing new software, nor is it necessarily possible to replicate the live, day-to-day trading environment exactly for testing purposes. Furthermore, players may be tempted to rush through final tests to meet delivery deadlines. In some smaller, more recent market entrants, release management protocols may not be fully developed.

Key Controls

As bad as the events we have discussed here may have seemed, the market may not yet have seen the worst-case scenario. To address this issue, good IT governance and safe IT release management practices are required from all players releasing software into the marketplace. This will, however, not be sufficient to prevent the reoccurrence of events such as we have recently seen.

Just like fire drills, people need to be told immediately when a situation is occurring and what to do when it does. Regulators, markets, investment banks, and other smaller players need to come together to discuss the different scenarios that have occurred and could occur in the future and develop a "break-the-glass" set of scenarios, plans, escalation procedures, and on/off switches for when they do. That would be a good start. Players also need to assess their strategic objectives and understand the risks for which they can have zero tolerance. If Knight Capital had done such risk assessment work, it perhaps could have put more focus into the sort of controls that underpinned its very existence.

Notes

1. On August 1, 2012, Knight Capital accidentally deployed test software code to a production environment. The test code was designed to move stock prices higher and lower in order to verify the behavior of trading algorithms in a controlled environment. When released into production, Knight's trading activities caused a major disruption in the prices of 148 companies listed at the New York Stock Exchange—thus, for example, shares of Wizzard Software Corporation went from $3.50 to $14.76.

2. The social networking company Facebook held its initial public offering (IPO) on Friday, May 18, 2012. The IPO was one of the biggest ever in technology, and the biggest in Internet history, with a peak market capitalization of over $104 billion. Trading was to begin at 11:00 a.m. However, trading was delayed until 11:30 a.m. due to technical problems with the NASDAQ exchange. Those early jitters would foretell ongoing problems, and the first day of trading was marred by numerous technical glitches that prevented orders from going through, or even confused investors as to whether or not their orders were successful.

3. The phrase *Big Bang,* used in reference to the sudden deregulation of financial markets, was coined to describe measures, including abolition of fixed commission charges and of the distinction between stockjobbers and stockbrokers on the London Stock Exchange and change from open-outcry to electronic, screen-based trading, enacted by the UK government in 1986. The day the London Stock Exchange's rules changed on October 27, 1986, was dubbed the Big Bang because of the increase in market activity expected from an aggregation of measures designed to alter the structure of the market.

4. Black Monday refers to Monday, October 19, 1987, when stock markets around the world crashed, shedding a huge value in a very short time. The crash began in Hong Kong and spread west to Europe, hitting the United States after other markets had already declined by a significant margin. The Dow Jones Industrial Average (DJIA) dropped by 508 points to 1738.74 (22.61 percent). A popular explanation was that the crash was caused by program traders. Economists such as Dean Furbush argued that the economy was as much to blame as technical market causes.

5. Established in 1971, NASDAQ was the world's first electronic stock market, though it originally operated as an electronic bulletin board.

6. In finance, a dark pool (also called a *black pool*) is a private forum for trading securities that is not openly available to the public. Liquidity on these markets is called *dark pool liquidity*. The bulk of dark pool trades represent large trades by financial institutions that are offered outside of public exchanges like the NYSE and the NASDAQ, so that such trades remain confidential and outside the purview of the general investing public. The fragmentation of financial trading venues and electronic trading has allowed dark pools to be created, and they are normally accessed through crossing networks or directly among market participants via private contractual arrangements.

7. Algorithmic trading, also called automated trading, black-box trading, or algo trading, is the use of electronic platforms for entering trading orders with an algorithm that executes preprogrammed trading instructions whose variables may include timing, price, or quantity of the order, or in many cases initiating the order by a "robot,"—in other words, without human intervention. Algorithmic trading is widely used by investment banks, pension funds, mutual funds, and other buy-side (investor-driven) institutional traders to divide large trades into several smaller trades to manage market impact and risk. Sell-side traders, such as market makers and some hedge funds, provide liquidity to the market, generating and executing orders automatically.

8. The May 6, 2010, Flash Crash, also known as The Crash of 2:45 and the 2010 Flash Crash, occurred when the Dow Jones Industrial Average plunged about 1000 points (about 9 percent) only to recover those losses within minutes. It was the second largest point swing, 1,010.14 points, and the biggest one-day point decline, 998.5 points, on an intraday basis in Dow Jones Industrial Average history.

9. A Senate investigation of the 2010 Flash Crash resulted in a report titled "Report Surrounding the Market Events of May 6th 2010" published on September 30, 2010. The report traced the causes of the event and outlines some solutions to prevent a reoccurrence.

10. The most recent proponent of the view that high-frequency trading has led to unfair market practices exploited by certain advantaged fast trading firms is Michael Lewis in *Flash Boys* (New York: W. W. Norton & Company, 2014).

11. The company attempted to go public on March 23, 2012, as the first listing on its own exchange, but later withdrew the IPO the same day due to a disastrous glitch in the company's trading systems. The glitch resulted in BATS's stock price falling from the original $16 offering price to as low as 4¢ a share. Three erroneous Apple trades on the BATS exchange triggered a circuit breaker, which temporarily halted trading in that stock. Those trades were later canceled. BATS halted stocks on its exchange that were affected by the glitch and included stocks with ticker symbols beginning with letters A to BFZZZ. It later reopened trading in the affected symbols but decided to withdraw the BATS stock offering. Following the failed IPO, the BATS board of directors decided to separate the roles of chairman and CEO. Joe Ratterman had held both roles. Ratterman received the "unanimous support" of the directors to keep the positions of CEO and president. In July 2012, BATS named Paul Atkins, a former SEC commissioner, to the role of nonexecutive chairman of its board of directors.

CHAPTER 9

Funding the Bad Guys—Winning the AML Battle

From a societal perspective, the risk of terrorist networks and drug traffickers utilizing the regulated financial system to launder money is likely the most important one faced by banks. Experts estimate that billions of dollars flow through the banking system from such sources every year, and thousands suffer as a result of the guns and drugs that the money buys. Large penalties and sanctions have been imposed on several of the largest banks for failures in this area.[1] In this chapter we trace the origins of anti–money laundering (AML) regulations, why they have not always worked as intended, and what can still be done to address these failures.

Modern Practices of Money Launderers and Undetected Cash Movers

A tremendous amount of money is moved around the world every year that is not part of the official flows of money. Such transactions take place through a number of ways, all of which are outlawed by various rules and regulations from tax to the US Office of Foreign Assets Control (OFAC) sanctions to anti–money laundering. If you are looking for why these transactions continue to take place, despite all the systems of controls put in place by regulators to prevent them, there is one reason: because someone wants these transactions to take place very badly. So badly that they will develop new types of schemes to make them happen.

Two examples have been covered extensively, but it is worthwhile describing them briefly to remind ourselves how hard it is to prevent these activities.

Banking secrecy is the first enabling example. It is a long-standing tenet of private banking and asset management in certain countries that client names be protected from the prying eyes of employees. Elaborate flows of money from a dictator in Africa or an oligarch in Russia through several intermediaries, possibly a private bank in Switzerland or Luxembourg, end up in an anonymous account in a hedge fund in New York (offshore in the Cayman Islands). A hedge fund manager might end up with the majority of his investors having an account in the name of a bank in Switzerland with no idea of who is behind that account. Meanwhile, the Know-Your_Client (KYC)[2] process that is supposed to review the identity documents of the investor is delayed because the account holder fails to produce the necessary documents. Finally, when the bank calls to close the account, the documents still have not been provided and may never be. In traditional private banks, customers remain anonymous, no address is held on file, and statements are kept at the bank for the customer should he ever bother to ask for them. Cash for deposit is in unmarked envelopes and concealed from view. In certain countries and cities, bankers might meet their clients in anonymous cafes where the transaction is conducted, possibly via an envelope that is passed under a newspaper. Accounts are numbered, and only the banker knows the identity of the account holder.

The second example of modern transactions based on avoiding tax or regulatory attention are executed by traders on behalf of intermediaries acting for a middleman acting for a dictator or an oligarch. One such class of transactions is known as *mirror trades*, which are back-to-back trades executed purely for the purposes of sending money abroad. A trader executes a customer order to buy a certain stock, let's say for a value of $10 million using Russian rubles. Following this, the trader executes a sale of the same stock on behalf of another company in exchange for dollars, euros, or pounds. Both companies have the same owner. Through the two transactions the owner has exchanged rubles for a foreign currency in a process that leaves no obvious trace to regulators.

So how would compliance identify such a scheme? First, trades have to be made repeatedly for no apparent purpose with purchase and sale of a security for no profit or a small loss. Second, if AML had been doing its job properly, the very close relationship between the entities buying and selling funds or intermediaries would have turned up in the checks and controls review. Third, at a macro level, if the volume of transactions was high enough, careful research might reveal schemes to squirrel away funds unofficially. Sometimes seeing the big picture can help to uncover the small sins of everyday life in banking. Looking at publicly available research to identify the amount of unofficial flows of money between countries can help to show that there is a problem, that there are schemes afoot to move money.

It is understandable, of course, why the modern methods of money laundering still include movements of cash in unmarked envelopes. It is a lot simpler to execute and still harder to detect. While changes in bank secrecy laws and regulations are in progress in some countries (e.g., the Swiss are repealing their secrecy laws that are intended to bring to account undeclared accounts), the people who want to move around money undetected will continue to try to do so. Surveillance methods will become increasingly important in the fight to prevent them from doing so.

Typically, the process of laundering money is a three-step process: placement, layering, and integration. In placement, illegitimate funds are introduced into the legitimate financial system. In layering, the money is moved around to create confusion, sometimes by wiring or transferring through different accounts. The separation of the funds from their source makes it harder to trace. Finally in integration, the money is integrated into the financial system through additional transactions until the "dirty money" appears clean and legitimate and easy to use and convert to other things that are needed. The way such funds are introduced into the system could be only a few steps removed from the terrorist or drug organization. Catching and identifying these movements requires help and support from governments and international cooperation between those with mutual interest in combating such activities.

Money Launderers and Terrorists

There has long been a nexus between terrorists and drug cartels. The terrorists provided security to the drug dealers in return for a cut of the action. Banks were the conduit for the flow of funds, and they were absolutely unprepared for the task of stopping them. There were no tools in place, no international agreements to cut off the flow of funds from region to region. Black September, the 1972 Olympics terrorist event, and plane hijackings such as that which led to the famous Raid on Entebbe were events that grabbed the headlines and necessitated an international response.

Legislature and Regulations

Tracking the money is not a simple task, but as early as 1970, legislation was enacted in the United States to combat money laundering. The Bank Secrecy Act (BSA) was passed in 1970 and established requirements for recordkeeping and reporting by private individuals, banks, and other financial institutions. The Act was designed to help identify the source, volume, and movement of currency and other monetary instruments transported or transmitted into or out of the United States or deposited in financial institutions. It also required banks to report cash transactions over $10,000 using the Currency Transaction Report, identify persons conducting transactions, and maintain a paper trail by keeping appropriate records of financial transactions. It was not, however, until the Money Laundering Control Act was passed in 1986 that money laundering was established as a federal crime. The Act, among other things, directed banks to establish and maintain procedures to ensure and monitor compliance with the reporting and recordkeeping requirements of the BSA.

These and measures acts passed in other countries tended to be piecemeal and parochial. Since the money launderers were active global networks, global tools and enforcement had to be, too.

A comprehensive, globally integrated approach was not attempted, however, until the founding of the Financial Action Task Force (FATF). The FATF was founded in 1989 by the G7 countries to counter the growing global threat of money laundering, efforts that gained momentum after 9/11. Under a framework established by the FATF, financial institutions globally, and many nonfinancial institutions, were obliged to identify and report transactions of a suspicious nature. A profession dedicated to building expertise and responsibility for oversight of AML controls grew as a result of the new regulations. Banks appointed managing directors to oversee AML compliance, with teams under them responsible for day-to-day execution. Compliance officers were charged with account monitoring and identifying sources of funds for transactions. All activities of the banks, from investment management to derivative trading to advisory, were subject to the requirement to know the customer and know the source of funds. Additionally, AML software was developed to filter customer data, classify it according to level of suspicion, and inspect it for anomalies. Any suspicious transactions were to be brought to management and a file reported with the government if management deemed it necessary.

Impact of Regulations

It is hard to say what impact these regulations have had in stymieing terrorists and drug traffickers, but the implications of the recent costly settlements between banks and regulators are that it has not been as much as one would have hoped. First, it is clear from the investigations conducted by the US Senate that banks have been severely resource constrained and have not always placed the most qualified staff in important roles in this area. Second, banks have, on occasion, differed from the regulators in their judgment of what constitutes a country of high risk. HSBC, for example, apparently identified Mexico as a country of low risk for money laundering (and therefore not subject to special surveillance) between 2000 and 2009, in contrast to the State Department's own assessment at the time. Third, investment banks and asset managers have at times gotten into sloppy habits and cut corners—for example, by allowing customers to defer production of documentation per AML requirements from the time they open the account to the time they close it. Leaving it to the time the customer chooses to close the account to require identification documents is too late. Fourth, reliance is not infrequently placed by traders, hedge funds, and asset managers on third parties, such as brokers and outsourced compliance officers to meet the requirements banks and asset managers have to meet under AML regulations. Fifth, based on the official wording from prosecution agreements by the Department of Justice over the past several years, there have been deliberate attempts to side step, even flout, the regulations designed to stop money laundering and terrorist funding.

It is not possible to catalog here all the failures and breakdowns of controls intended to prevent money laundering but regulators' investigations into money laundering activities taking place at major banks resulted in major settlements and large fines within a broad scope of violations by major banks (see Table 9-1).

An Effective AML Program

Following these regulatory investigations, fines, and required changes imposed on banks, structured reviews of their AML programs have been

Table 9-1 Largest Fines Imposed for AML Failures

Firm	Fine (in US billions)	Year
BNP Paribas	~$9	2015
HSBC	~$2	2012
CSFB	~$0.5	2012
ABN AMRO	~$0.5	2010
Wachovia	~$0.2	2010

forced on those found culpable. Additional resources have been applied to these programs dedicated to combating money laundering and terrorist financing, which have to address each stage in the banking process: first, when a client becomes a client; second, when the client transacts; and third, when the client stops being a client.

The following diagram indicates the life cycle and the interlocking activities.

Customer Due Diligence → Pre-Transaction

→ Post-Transaction → Risk Assessment

Customer Due Diligence

When a new customer comes on board the bank, under the terms of the "know your customer" requirements of the 2001 Patriot Act, each line of business must develop and maintain procedures for identifying the customer's background, risk profile, and so on per KYC requirements. The bank's due diligence on each customer should be sufficient as to enable it to develop an understanding of normal and expected activity for the customer's occupation or business operations.

Once the client is on-boarded, business units should have policies and procedures regarding the updating of customer's due-diligence information. Such updates should be performed as part of a periodic and routine basis, confirming that customer activity is conforming to expectations and the identity information is still good. In addition, procedures need to be in place to ensure events such as change of ownership, the addition of higher-risk products or location, or unusual transaction activity result in updates to customer information.

Banks also need a process to off-board clients or other entities in both voluntary and involuntary situations. The process associated with voluntary off-boarding is a process known as de-risking. De-risking decisions can be made vis-à-vis products, countries, whole businesses, or clients on the basis of observations or evidence of suspicious activities. In the case of a client, a decision to exit a relationship would typically be made or discussed in a specific country and line of business where the relationship exists. In the case of a global bank, such suspicions should be shared across countries and lines of business while complying with privacy regulations, and ensure that any de-risking is coordinated effectively.

The problem for large universal banks is that bad actors can pop up in different branches of the bank all over the globe. An effective AML program should be able to triangulate its records across the globe to ensure a single customer relationship file. As banks build electronic databases that can make customer information available to relationship managers in any country, however, they need to ensure they do not fall afoul of data privacy and bank secrecy laws in the different countries in which they operate. While the United States wants to operate global search activities, individual countries' privacy laws may not necessarily cooperate. Firms need to ensure that they understand those privacy laws and stay within compliance.

Pre-Transaction Screening

It is possible, of course, that bad actors can slip through the net, and that once-good actors turned bad clients can create unwitting victims of launderers and other wrongdoers. Banks need to guard against this by screening all transactions against certain criteria and lists of sanctioned or bad actors. The US Office of Foreign Assets Control (OFAC), for instance, maintains a list of entities, including countries, organizations, and individuals, that it is illegal for US companies to do business with. Other countries maintain similar types of lists, and thus global banks have to take these into account also. There are three levels of sanctions:

- Level 1—global list from the UN
- Level 2—regional lists—from the European Union, for instance
- Level 3—country-based lists[3]

Compliance for global banks is far from easy where there are conflicts potentially between US lists and other operating country lists. Russia is an example where the United States imposed sanctions on certain Russian individuals and then Russia followed suit. So for a US bank based in Russia, it will be a case of damned if you do, damned if you don't. Of course, no one said that running a global bank was easy, but it may be getting harder. The likes of Germany, Hong Kong, and the United Kingdom all have sanctions regimes in place every bit as rigorous as OFAC. The UK treasury, for instance, has over 9,000 entities on its list.

The implementation challenges for a global bank's pre-transaction screening are multiplied by the sheer volume of transactions going through and the number of locations and business units those transactions travel through. Typically, banks have built systems in different locations in response to in-country legislation and requirements. The challenge now is to create a globally consistent operating model that screens out the vast number of false negatives and escalates to regional and global compliance in an appropriate and timely manner. This should ensure identification of confirmed hits with lists and escalation in a short timescale.

Although there are some very sophisticated systems out there, putting in place the right business process and high-quality data are the most significant challenges. The key challenges here are to ensure consistency, completeness, and precision of sanction screening, completeness of sources for payments and messages, and creating real-time reporting and analytics to key decision makers. Again, underlying all this is making sure that the bank respects privacy and bank secrecy laws. Can OFAC-blocked transaction reports, for example, be shared with the US regulator if the activity originated in, say, China? Banks need to make sure they stay up to date with the privacy, bank secrecy, and regulatory laws in each operating country to ensure ongoing compliance.

Post-Transaction Monitoring

Banks need to also monitor for suspicious activity once transactions have been posted, activity not necessarily anticipated in the due-diligence process or matched in the pre-transaction screening process. The ultimate outputs of this monitoring are suspicious activity or transaction reports (SARs, STRs).[4] Different countries impose different filling requirements, but the basic requirement is a common one. The first part of the process is feeding transactions into a tool that can mine the data for scenarios that suggest suspicious activities. Examples might include cash coming in and out of accounts for no obvious business purpose; cash coming in from high risk or unusual locations; or cash transactions of an unusual size relative to the norm for the particular customer. Once suspicions are identified, alerts are generated for the investigation team to investigate and determine if a report or more drastic action is merited.

Like with pretrade screening, banks will generally have built over time different systems and processes across the globe. The implementation challenge again is to create a globally consistent operating model while taking advantage of global or regional centers of modeling and investigative excellence.

Once an SAR/STR has been filed in any country, US banks are expected to ensure that such international SARs are shared with their US home office to identify if there is a nexus of bad behavior. Again, banks need to research privacy and bank secrecy laws to ensure they are legally entitled under the country's privacy laws from sharing the information outside the country. Banks have been found wanting in this space by regulators—hence, the number of consent orders, fines, and so on. It is clear from such regulatory actions that management needs to ensure that adequate staffing, information quality, and consistent standards are maintained for disposition of alerts of suspicious activity and appropriate escalation to senior control officers at the bank. Dedicated teams are needed in the areas of scenario modeling, alert disposition and follow-up, case investigators, quality testing, and reporting analytics to ensure full compliance. The investment that is required in this space is significant.

Risk Assessment

Banks are also required to conduct AML and sanctions risk assessments. Customers or entities should be risk ranked based on factors such as geography, customer type, products and services used, and account activity. Customers deemed to be high risk should be subject to closer scrutiny, with transactions involving high-risk jurisdictions and unusual account activity subject to additional analysis. Key factors are:

- Country risk—identifying geographic locations that pose a higher risk for money laundering is essential in any AML program. External vendors can be leveraged for country risk analysis.
- Industry risk—by the nature of their business or occupation, certain customers and entities pose unique money laundering and terrorist financing risk. Specialist guidance should be provided to employees working in such areas.
- Product risk—specific guidance on products and services that are considered to present a high risk for money laundering should be provided to employees. Typically, such products include correspondent banking, prepaid cards, mobile banking, and remote deposit.

The output of this activity should be an assessment of the level of risk and the adequacy of controls, including risks associated with each line of business and enterprise-wide. Banks need to satisfy themselves and regulators that they have effective assessment methods and execution capabilities. Many banks divide the assessment into two aspects: quantitative and qualitative. In an effective program, it is useful to triangulate the results from both to ensure they are reasonable and can detect data issues. Quantitative typically leverages product, client, and transaction data, while qualitative methods deploy surveys of business owners to leverage their views of risk in their particular domains.

Mitigating the Risk

Besides making improvements to these AML programs, how can this risk be better mitigated? First, training and education is key. Too often, banks and asset managers simply view AML requirements as overhead. They need to educate staff to better understand the reason for the controls and the consequences of failing to implement them effectively—that is, the damage wrought by terrorists and by drugs on real people. Second, banks should use judgment and third-party services to determine the risk and then use efficient ways to monitor for it. This likely means employing staff and vendors with expertise in country risk, international relations, and international law enforcement. Greater familiarity and passion for understanding the way that international networks move their funds around the globe will help better tailor an effective response to stop them. Third, armed with this expertise, invest in analytical and cognitive surveillance tools and software to leverage big data to detect more quickly potential networks and suspicious patterns of money movements and link together apparently unlinked accounts. Artificial intelligence and cognitive capabilities, such as machine learning and natural language processing, can be applied to networks and activities to identify anomalous connections, coded communications, and suspicious transactions. Fourth, being successful in this battle will also require greater cooperation between banks and law enforcement.

Notes

1. AML settlements with major banks:

    ■ *US v. HSBC Bank USA NA et al.,* US District Court, Eastern District of New York, No. 12-cr-00763. The judge in the case in July 2013 approved HSBC Holdings

Plc's (HSBA.L) HBC.N record $1.92 billion settlement with federal and state investigators of charges that it flouted rules designed to stop money laundering and thwart transactions with countries under US sanctions. The settlement resolved charges accusing HSBC of having degenerated into a "preferred financial institution" for Mexican and Colombian drug cartels, money launderers, and other wrongdoers through what the US Department of Justice called "stunning failures of oversight." HSBC acknowledged compliance lapses, including a failure to maintain an effective AML program, and conducting transactions on behalf of customers in Burma, Cuba, Iran, Libya, and Sudan, which were all subject to US sanctions. https://www.justice.gov/opa/pr/hsbc-holdings-plc-and-hsbc-bank-usa-na-admit-anti-money-laundering-and-sanctions-violations.

- Standard Chartered, which has acknowledged some wrongdoing in the matter, agreed to pay $327 million in fines to US regulators in December 2012. That's on top of the $340 million it agreed to pay after New York Superintendent of Financial Services Benjamin Lawsky lambasted the bank in August 2012, a move that caught the bank and other regulators off guard. The allegations accused the fifth-biggest UK bank by assets of illegally scheming over a decade to move some $200 million through the US system, money that the regulators say the Iranian embargoes don't allow. https://www.justice.gov/opa/pr/standard-chartered-bank-agrees-forfeit-227-million-illegal-transactions-iran-sudan-libya-and.

- According to the press release from the Department of Justice on May 1 2015, BNP Paribas was sentenced for conspiring to violate the International Emergency Economic Powers Act (IEEPA) and the Trading with the Enemy Act (TWEA) by processing billions of dollars of transactions through the U.S. financial system on behalf of Sudanese, Iranian and Cuban entities subject to U.S. economic sanctions. Also included in the press release was this direct quote: "BNPP, the world's fourth largest bank, has now been sentenced to pay a record penalty of almost $9 billion for sanctions violations that unlawfully opened the U.S. financial markets to Sudan, Iran, and Cuba," said U.S. Attorney Bharara. "BNPP provided access to billions of dollars to these sanctioned countries, and did so deliberately and secretly, in ways designed to evade detection by the U.S. authorities." https://www.justice.gov/opa/pr/bnp-paribas-sentenced-conspiring-violate-international-emergency-economic-powers-act-and.

2. Know-Your-Customer requirements. Under the legislation passed by Congress, banks and other financial institutions are required to undertake certain checks of new and existing customers to verify that they are who they purport to be. Such checks include obtaining copies of identification documents such as passports and drivers licenses.

3. List screening. Under the rules of OFAC, firms are required to screen client transactions against lists of sanctioned entities. If a match between one of the sanctioned

entities and the transaction is made, certain reports need to be filed with OFAC. Other countries maintain similar lists and have similar requirements.

4. Under AML legislation in the United States and other countries, financial firms are required to file SARs (Suspicious Activity Reports) in the United States or STRs (Suspicious Transaction Reports) in countries outside the United States. Several international banks were charged with failures to execute all their obligations under such legislation in the past several years and so the number of SARs and STRs filed in the past is unlikely to be an accurate representation of such activity.

CHAPTER 10

Litigation and Big Data Risk

Another significant operational risk faced by investment banks is from litigation following deals or public securities issuance that turned sour. In such cases, bankers, along with accountants, are frequent targets for blame. How can this risk be effectively mitigated?

What Is the Risk?

The cost of litigation faced by investment banking, most commonly on the equity and loan underwriting side, is one of the highest potential costs from operational risk across an investment bank's key lines of business. That is because when a company fails, investors who bought into the most recent stock or debt offering will naturally feel aggrieved at the unexpected turn of events and the resultant loss they suffered. In their grief they will ask questions and sometimes take the view, like it or not, that were it not for the incompetence of the bankers, they would still be whole.

A conspicuous number of the litigation settlements of the past few years are related to actions stemming from the 2008 Financial Crisis because of the sudden collapse of many firms due to the onset of the crisis. A firm that has collapsed is an inherent danger to its bankers as it lashes out in its final death throes. The common complaint from an investment bank's risk managers is that they are typically targeted as a result of having deep pockets rather than due to any wrongdoing on their part (see Table 10-1).

One of the ways to protect against this risk is an executed engagement letter and broad indemnification clause. This is, of course, the standard approach to contracting in the United States: Provide a service, get paid for it, and then protect oneself against litigation in the event that the service is less than what was expected by the client. It is also perfectly rational to protect your business, however, given the litigious society we live in. It is expected for aggrieved investors to assert that their bankers should have known anything and

Table 10-1 Largest Settlements with Shareholders' Lawsuits

Case	Loss (in US billions)	Year	Defendants
Enron	~$7	2004	Several global banks
WorldCom	~$6	2005	Several global banks
Merrill Lynch	~$2.4	2012	Bank of America

everything about the company they are underwriting. In practice, this is impossible, and so in this context, the indemnity tool and engagement letter that spell out the scope of services are critical tools in reducing the cost of any settlements in negotiation or court.

On occasion, owing to "relationship" or "politics" or sloppiness on the part of the team, bankers do not always execute an engagement and indemnification letter. Good practice dictates the use of workflow tools to track production and execution of these documents. Investment bankers tend to work in more unstructured environments and investment is not always forthcoming in the sort of workflow and document management tools that make this easier to manage. Unfortunately, it only takes sloppy practices in one region of a global bank to create an issue.

The second key control to protecting against this risk is conducting due diligence on the company being acquired or underwritten. Due diligence comprises a review of the company by the bankers. This should include review of financial and management assets to help ensure that the buyer and shareholder are getting what they think they are getting. Over the years, due diligence has been managed on a fairly informal basis, but increasingly, risk managers have tried to move bankers toward a checklist, more formalized approach. Additional aspects, such as environmental risks, have also been introduced to the process in recognition of the fact that damage to the environment can be a subject of lawsuits, with potential consequences for advisors. Due diligence should be limited to the investment bankers' responsibilities and scope of expertise.

In addition, bankers should seek to minimize conflicts by ensuring independence in this process. One problematic but occasional practice has been for banks making an acquisition to appoint themselves as lead bankers in the deal. Due diligence is normally conducted by the leader in the deal, and the perceived conflict may be problematic should the acquisition be later litigated. The $6 billion Lehman bond offering that was led by Lehman Brothers shortly before its collapse in 2008 was one such deal. Members of the syndicate later settled with shareholders who claimed that advisers failed to disclose a catalog of important matters, such as high-risk residential mortgage-lending practices, increasing concentration of mortgage-related risks, and allegedly inaccurate financial statements. Details of these alleged failures can be found at http://lehmansecuritieslitigation.com/.

The third risk control is a document management system that ensures all key documents are retained and organized effectively. When lawsuits are brought, documents need to be produced on demand, similar to if regulators demand documents. Engagement letters, for example, generally go through many different versions, and computer files end up with multiple versions. Therefore, it is essential to maintain discipline and systems to be able to access the final version executed by both parties. Bankers have in the past at least generally worked on deals without effective document management tools—for example, saving documents on their hard drives without saving to a common shared folder. In the past, banks have not necessarily had effective ways of storing and archiving data and documents so that they can be retrieved quickly and efficiently. A federal judge awarded significant punitive damages against Morgan Stanley in the 2005 Sunbeam case for allegedly failing to produce documents.[1] Although the ruling was subsequently overturned, banks have since taken steps to shore up controls in this area. Document management and managing the life cycle of data effectively is an important tool in the arsenal of banks in this time of massive data volumes.

Systemic Risks from Big Data

The underlying problem for banks comes back to data and the sheer amount of it. According to a 2011 McKinsey study, "90% of the data in the world was created in the last two years."[2] Most experts believe that for most organizations, the volume of data will double every two years. There is significant operational risk associated with this increase in data as demonstrated by the increases in litigation from investors and state and federal regulators over the past decade. That has been coupled with a general increase in regulatory curiosity, as evidenced by the increase in examinations visited upon banks on a routine and extraordinary basis, mortgages, LIBOR, and FX, to name a few of the more recent examples. In the case of the LIBOR investigations, one large bank estimated that its internal systems retrieved 100 million documents and reviewed them using 1,000 different search terms, according to a March 2014

Financial Times article.[3] Careful risk management is needed to address two related aspects of the parallel increase in data and litigation:

1. Banks have to manage the process carefully by which data and evidence required by litigants and regulators are retained and collected.
2. Banks have to review their stored data in relation to legal and business criticality retention requirements.

Whatever data, then, that do not need to be retained, should, as a general rule, not be kept and banks can save money and reduce risk accordingly. Most, however, have failed to dispose of unnecessary data accumulated over the last decade and have excess applications, servers, data, backups, storage, and tapes that no longer have any utility but that add cost and risk. Fines have been imposed by regulators on banks, which have proven unable to retain and dispose of its data within a well-ordered governance and legal framework. A rather different case is that of Arthur Andersen and the alleged attempt that was made to delete email evidence. The deletion of old data can be legitimate, of course, if it is managed within a published archive and deletion schedule. Emails deleted within that context of a broader policy framework can be legitimately defended. Without such a framework, deletion of emails can appear suspicious and difficult to defend against.

When lawyers set out on the process of litigating a case only a few decades ago, before the advent of email, the process was very different. Identifying and collecting evidence was a matter of combing through physical documents. Today, while the volume of documents to review has gone up considerably, the process of mining documents for relevant information is far easier due to computer technology and keyword search techniques used to identify the relevant data and information, known as eDiscovery.

There are, however, still many obstacles to making the process efficient and fail-safe. First, once a new case has been brought, there must be a process for ensuring that all related information and data are put on hold (i.e., not deleted). The process also requires that such individuals confirm receipt of the hold request and that they will comply with its requirements. For a large and complex company, this can be challenging because it is not always clear who is a party to an action—people leave and new people arrive, and computer hardware gets replaced, all of which make it hard to keep track. Second, relevant data must be identified and then retained until the case is closed, which again needs to be tracked and then acted upon at the appropriate time. That is far from straightforward, and, furthermore, for banks that have retained data that could have been deleted from a legal and business perspective, its continued retention can pose additional risk by making it subject to litigation where it need not have been.

What should banks be doing to address the costs and risks associated with storing its data? Banks need to build discipline around the information lifecycle and the process of deleting data that are no longer required from a legal and business standpoint. This is more complex than it sounds, since different types of documents are subject to different legal and regulatory retention requirements. Given this complexity, it behooves banks to ensure that they have access to an authoritative source of laws and regulations for each country they do business in and link their retention schedules to that legal and regulatory framework. Such a link should be clearly documented and traceable within a database that is internal to the bank. This process, known as *defensible disposal,* can help to ensure that banks can justify their data deletions to regulators, judges, litigants, and other interested parties. Second, banks should consider tools to support the eDiscovery process and its associated requirements—for example, by automating the process of notifying the custodians of the data that are subject to legal hold; automating the confirmations that they will abide by the request; and automating the process of identifying and retaining the data that are associating with the case. Furthermore, banks should put in place a central repository for storing all types of communication to enable the rapid retrieval of such communication pertaining to new cases and regulatory enquiries. The availability of increased computing power and modern elastic search capabilities makes this possible even for the largest universal banks with several hundred thousand employees and over 50 different communication channels.[4]

Deploying these various tools and techniques linked to information life cycle governance and eDiscovery will help reduce both storage costs and operational risk exposure. Like the adoption of any tools and processes that involve change, this is hard to do, but in the long run it should pay off.

Notes

1. *Morgan Stanley v. Sunbeam 2005*: In June 2004, a Morgan Stanley technology executive signed a court document certifying he had handed over all emails the firm had agreed to produce in a suit filed against his firm by billionaire financier Ronald Perelman. But two weeks earlier, the executive, Arthur Riel, hadn't been so sure.

"The storage folks found an additional 1,600 backup tapes in a closet," Mr. Riel told two Morgan Stanley lawyers, he recalled in a deposition quoted in court papers. The tapes hadn't been searched for emails before Mr. Riel signed the document, the firm acknowledged in court. To the Florida state judge overseeing the case, Mr. Riel's certification was false and one of many instances in which Morgan Stanley "deliberately" violated her orders to turn over documents, including some embarrassing to one of the firm's bankers. As a result of what she described as Morgan Stanley's "bad faith" actions, Judge Elizabeth Maass made an extraordinary legal decision: She told the jury it should simply assume the firm helped defraud Mr. Perelman. Mr. Perelman sought $2.7 billion after Morgan Stanley rejected his offer to settle for $20 million. The firm had already set aside $360 million to cover potential damages, and, according to court transcripts, regulators looked into whether the firm's conduct violated federal laws.

2. James Manyika, Michael Chui, Brad Brown, Jacques Bughin, Richard Dobbs, Charles Roxburgh, Angela Hung Byers, "Big Data: The Next Frontier for Innovation, Competition and Productivity," McKinsey & Company (May 2011), http://www.mckinsey.com/business-functions/digital-mckinsey/our-insights/big-data-the-next-frontier-for-innovation.

3. *Financial Times* (March 2014).

4. The growth of communication channels has been immense in the past decade. Where before, compliance was monitoring email and phone calls, add to that now internal chat applications, internal social media communication channels, Bloomberg chat, Reuters chat, and others. Also, banks allow certain employees to establish an official presence on Facebook, LinkedIn, and other channels so that these need to be monitored, also. In addition, banks have been establishing dedicating chat rooms between themselves and major clients, so these need to be added to the mix.

CHAPTER 11

Twitter Risk and Fake News Risk

Fake news is all the rage now. But this is not a new phenomenon. Just a week after the SEC announced its decision in early 2013 to loosen restrictions on the use of Twitter and other social media by companies, a hacker showed how risky a decision that could prove to be. When an Associated Press Twitter account announced to the world that the White House was under attack, the reaction from the financial market was instantaneous. The Dow declined 150 points and several billion dollars of market value was wiped out in a few seconds. It turns out the AP's Twitter account had been hacked, but the damage was done. This was not a scenario that was predicted but now it was one firms cannot choose to ignore.

Just as with the AP scenario, every Twitter and Facebook account is potentially a target. Were any public company's Twitter account to be hacked and incorrect news about earnings, acquisitions, sales, or other information released to the world, it would potentially have an instantaneous impact on the market. Unlike news of an attack on the White House, a false earnings report or proposed merger might not be so easy to quickly prove to be false to the world at large. As we move headlong into the instant-news-cycle-driven world, firms should take a step back to evaluate the risk that this poses. Institutions must evaluate the risk posed by the proliferation of official firm social media accounts. Such proliferation multiplies the threat posed not just by external misuse, highlighted by recent incidents, but also internal or rogue misuse.

There is one thing that can be observed in any organization that uses information technology to any extent: The number of user accounts in applications that are useful and easy to use will see exponential growth and rapid proliferation unless a concerted effort is made to exert control over the process. A common example is just the process of creating folders on shared drives to house documents. Since they are free and easy to create, hundreds of folders containing data are accessible to every employee who authors or edits Word, Excel, or PowerPoint files. Some of these may contain important, privileged information; the bulk, however, will not. How does a firm ensure the ability to identify and protect the latter from inappropriate dissemination? Alternatively, when a judge demands documents, how does a firm ensure it is able to locate and provide them? Attempts to exert central control generally come too late to be effective. A plan needs to be formulated upfront.

If banks need to worry about the control over the proliferation of internal accounts and unstructured data sources, how much more so for accounts on web applications that house and relay information to the public domain? Apps, such as Twitter, are free to use: no expensive licensing deals with named, authorized users are required. The risk is further increased since Twitter, Facebook, and other social media platforms have been sanctioned for use by the SEC and management as a means of broadcasting market-sensitive information. One imagines that each line of business will soon want its own account to broadcast its progress to the outside world. One wonders how many official Twitter accounts each major bank already has. With the media reporting on how boring these corporate Twitter accounts can be, one can imagine that the shackles of corporate control may be loosened to make things more interesting. After all, what is the point of having a Twitter account if it has no followers? To get followers, one needs to be interesting, even newsworthy. The natural tendency to try to gain an edge in the competitive brokerage, trading, and investment world through passing on interesting information to clients and potential clients may become harder to police as accounts proliferate and become part of a normative sales and business development strategy. As well as monitoring the tweets and updates of those who are authorized to use Twitter on behalf of the company, how does one monitor those who are not authorized to do so when there are many such accounts? More fundamentally, how does one ensure that all material information that is distributed by such channels is distributed broadly enough to satisfy Fair Disclosure Rules?[1]

Not only can "official" corporate Twitter or Facebook accounts be cause for concern, personal accounts can be as well. In this increasingly narcissistic "selfie" world we live in, the silly story of former Representative Anthony

Weiner may turn out to be the canary in the coal mine. It turns out that not just politicians but CEOs and other high-flying and ambitious executives are shameless self-promoters. Furthermore, a conflation of corporate identity with personal identity is likely to occur when any cyber moment can be turned into a branding opportunity. And when the brand of the CEO becomes the brand of the company, or indeed when anyone's personal brand can be so intertwined, then it can be argued that the personal and the corporate have been melded into one. At that point, is there anything distinctly personal and private anymore? So companies may need to monitor activities on employees' Facebook pages to ensure that their brands are being promoted rather than dirtied. A senior executive or CEO updating pictures on his Facebook page with racy pictures in a luxury resort or in a newly purchased $50 million home may send out the wrong message to customers. A CEO tweeting negative remarks about gay marriage may conflict with corporate values. Yet even more concerning would be a CEO sending out information or opinions on the state of the company to his friend on Facebook. Yet privacy laws can be problematic here because in many countries, companies are forbidden from monitoring their employees' personal social media accounts.

Firms can get ahead of this issue by providing clear rules of the road on the use of social media, whether with personal or corporate accounts. Firms need to make sure they have adequate "code red" or "break the glass" procedures in place for when a false report is issued from a firm account. As we saw with the AP tweet about the White House, the market reacts incredibly quickly and, though a firm may be held blameless for a hacked account, it may not be if it fails to alert the market in a timely way. With regard to personal accounts used by senior executives and CEOs, this is already a highly effective means of promoting personal and corporate brands. Firms need to make sure they have an appropriate framework in place for educating, monitoring, and responding to events caused by their misuse, intentional or otherwise.

Note

1. Fair Disclosure, also commonly referred to as Regulation FD or Reg FD, is a regulation promulgated by the SEC in August 2000. The rule mandates that all publicly traded companies must disclose material information to all investors

at the same time. The regulation sought to stamp out selective disclosure, in which some investors (often large institutional investors) received market-moving information before others (often smaller, individual investors). Regulation FD fundamentally changed how companies communicate with investors by bringing more transparency and more frequent and timely communications, perhaps more than any other regulation in the history of the SEC.

CHAPTER 12

Spreadsheet Risk: Should We Ban Excel?

Anyone working with spreadsheets knows how useful and indispensable they can be. At the same time, it is also well known how easy it is to make an error, perhaps in an embedded formula or a cell reference. A colleague of mine who works in the area of financial model risk has spent a good deal of time and money fixing spreadsheets that have errors in them—errors that can have significant impact on financial results and public reporting of financial results. This chapter looks at this risk and what can be done to mitigate it.

In 2013, we learned that spreadsheet errors may also have been indirectly responsible for extending the financial crisis in Europe a year or two longer than it might have otherwise been. It was discovered that a spreadsheet error was behind the results of a study that was influential in the setting of austerity measures in Europe post financial crisis.[1] These measures, albeit indirectly, led to job losses across Europe and the United States. If these losses occurred as a result of an influential piece of research that was based on a spreadsheet error, this surely qualifies as a very significant operational risk event.

So what happened exactly? Two Harvard professors, Carmen Reinhart and Kenneth Rogoff, wrote a research paper in 2010 called "Growth in a Time of Debt." The paper by two very well-known and respected economists claimed that there was a close correlation between a country's growth rates and a country's debt level where it exceeded 90 percent of gross domestic product (GDP). Though the professors say they never made the claim that the relationship was a directly causal one, it did not stop others from drawing that conclusion. Indeed, policy makers in Europe and the United States widely cited the study in prescribing austerity measures aimed at bringing down debt levels.

Other economists, however, in reviewing the research results were unable to recreate the results. Finally, after a research team at the University of

Massachusetts revisited the data and recently published its results, it became clear why that is.[2] The key finding, that countries with over 90 percent debt have negative growth rates, is only obtained when certain important data points are excluded. Furthermore, it seems that some of these data points were excluded because a formula in the spreadsheet did not include certain rows of data. The new study specifically obtained the correlation claimed by Rogoff and Reinhart by excluding Australia, Austria, Canada, and Denmark. Once these data were included, the authors of the new study showed the average growth rate for countries with over 90 percent debt ratio is actually 2.2 percent.

So can we say that this spreadsheet error led mistakenly to austerity measures that, in turn, have needlessly led to millions of job losses in Europe and elsewhere? Of course, there were many economists and policy makers in favor of austerity measures and the importance of maintaining low debt levels well before this paper was published. No lesser a figure than Margaret Thatcher would have been an honorary member of such a group, for example. There were also other well-known flaws in the Rogoff-Reinhart arguments that policy makers chose to ignore when citing Rogoff-Reinhart's study in support of austerity measures—for instance, that the low growth rate preceded the high debt level rather than vice-versa. At the same time, the episode is another reminder of the operational risks inherent in Excel and other spreadsheet programs. Firms that spend hundreds of millions of dollars in new technology annually have pockets of the firm reliant on formulae hidden in obscure, nestled spreadsheets. Yes, it would be nice to ban Excel from such uses, but unfortunately, ease of use and flexibility make it strangely addictive. In this context, firms should continue to apply resources to identify and ensure close oversight of any spreadsheets that inform the firms' books and records or any other key production data. Furthermore, continued migration from such dependencies should be part of this continuing effort. Economists should do the same.

Mitigating the Risk

Unlike a small team of research economists, large investment banks deploy spreadsheets in very large numbers across a number of functions. Though it is well known that Excel is highly error prone and is not suitable for use as part of a mission-critical information system, it very often is. While information officers and business partners yearly repeat their mantra that they will replace spreadsheets with appropriate enterprise platforms, spreadsheets have a habit of wiggling their way back in. There have been many examples in the last few years of functions having a critical dependency on a spreadsheet that was implicated in an operational risk mishap of one sort or another. Such incidents have included: misreporting of the value of a financial asset,[3] misreporting of a valuation at risk (VaR) model,[4] and misreporting of various credit models used to calculate credit capital calculations for the federal banks stress tests.[5] Behind all these incidents is the continued use of Excel for present-value calculations, profit and loss analysis, VaR modeling, complex security and positions valuations, and many other uses. The proliferation demonstrates that it is impossible to contain the spread or use of spreadsheets—they are simply too useful, too flexible to ignore. Thousands and thousands of spreadsheets can be found on the networks and hard drives of analysts and traders, some of them developed on the fly, others incorporating sophisticated programming and code. Some of the spreadsheets contain significant outright errors; others may contain small errors that can change in significance, depending on the data. Many investment banks alerted by the significant impact of errors in spreadsheets impacting regulatory submissions, including quarterly financial statements released to the public, have started to put in place programs to mitigate the damage. The first step in such programs is to identify the purpose of each spreadsheet that is in use. It is important to distinguish between spreadsheets that impact or help to calculate the books and records of the firm or contribute toward the calculation of the market risk that the firm carries versus spreadsheets that help bankers make investment decisions. The second step is to identify spreadsheets that include complex formulae and code. Once you have isolated these "high-risk" user tools, you can put in place a remediation program aimed at identifying errors in the code or in the formulae. This is no simple task, but putting in place such steps is an important part of any operational risk remediation program. There are tools available today that can help to automate this prioritization and error identification process and should be utilized wherever possible.

Notes

1. The 27 EU member states aimed to cut deficits by a maximum of 3 percent of GDP through 2014–2015 according to a May 2012 BBC report. Severe austerity measures were established in Europe following the Great Recession with the view that such measures would support a return to economic growth. http://www.bbc.com/news/10162176

2. Thomas Herndon, Michael Ash, and Robert Pollin, "Does High Public Debt Consistently Stifle Economic Growth? A Critique of Reinhart and Rogoff," *Cambridge Journal of Economics* 38, no. 2 (December 2013), pp. 257–279.

3. Credit Suisse financial reporting restatement—2008: The SEC charged four former veteran investment bankers and traders at Credit Suisse with engaging in a complex scheme to fraudulently overstate the prices of $3 billion in subprime bonds during the height of the subprime credit crisis. Kareem Serageldin, the former Credit Suisse trader, and three other traders admitted to mismarking their positions to avoid losses in their investment portfolio at the end of 2007. The use of Excel spreadsheets was at the center of the scandal, being used to validate favorable prices from favorable pricing sources. The lack of controls over the spreadsheet that was used to validate pricing was a critical point of failure in this case.

4. A spreadsheet model was widely faulted for the errors in the mathematical model used to calculate the VaR of the positions held during the so-called London Whale episode in April and May 2012, in which JPMorgan trader Bruno Iksil (nicknamed the London Whale), lost about $2 billion in credit default swaps.

5. Many major banks have failed to report credit capital adequately under Comprehensive Capital Analysis and Review requirements introduced after the financial crisis. The most recent of these was the error made by Bank of America in 2014. The use of spreadsheets to help with these calculations has been notorious for being behind many of these failures.

CHAPTER 13

Acts of God Risk

In the aftermath of Superstorm Sandy[1] in 2012, various articles pointed out the gap between the size of the storm's surge and the magnitude of such an outlying event planned for by New York City and coastal New Jersey. What was expected was much smaller than what was delivered by nature. For business continuity plans and overall infrastructure, the storm aftermath led to the question of whether said plans were effective, given existing storm data and forecasted trends for potential future storms. How do we plan more effectively for such events in the future? Scenario analysis offers one useful approach.

Industry and its infrastructure have, of course, always been vulnerable to catastrophes, both manmade and nature-based. The impacts of terrorism, earthquakes, and fraud have all impacted industry in the past decade. The problem of determining the likelihood and impact of a terrorist attack, a large oil spill, or a massive hurricane like Sandy is inherently hard to solve for. However, it is a critical step to take if one is to appropriately address each type of risk. Overestimating the size and frequency of future events can result in wasted resources. Yet, natural inertia, ingrained optimism, and pressure of the day to day can lead to a fatal failure for disaster planning to keep up with the level of potential danger as it ebbs and flows. In reviewing many business continuity plans of firms impacted by Superstorm Sandy, it is clear that this is what happened in this case.

There is clearly a need to strike the right balance between wasted resources and much-needed investment in preventive or mitigating systems. One useful tool developed to address this issue is risk scenario planning. In broad terms, such planning assesses alternate scenarios of how things could go very badly wrong in the future. These scenarios are subject to discussion and dialogue between subject matter experts and organization budget managers in a workshop setting. Data are brought to the table to frame the discussion, including case studies of past events and their associated impacts. While having a good understanding of what happened in the past is critical, it is not sufficient for imagining, in the context of a dynamic, constantly changing system, what could go wrong in the future. A more accurate forecast depends on an honest appraisal of the effectiveness of those things put in place to prevent or to mitigate future events—and ideally, other information that sheds light on the current likelihood or impact of future events. In the context of volatile weather, this could be broad trends on ocean levels, size and frequency of hurricanes potentially in the path of the city, and the strength of safeguards put in place to prevent or mitigate the damage to a firm's physical and network infrastructure.

The real power of scenario planning is based on two somewhat qualitative and behavioral aspects. First, taking leaders and subject matter experts away from the day-to-day exigencies of their work allows them to focus on those risks that have the power to take away their work on a permanent basis.

Second, giving space and opportunity for the imagination to crawl through the data, visualize real scenarios that could happen, and honestly evaluate those things that have been put in place to prevent or mitigate such events is surprisingly underestimated as a management tool. The absence of that opportunity can lead to an absence of imagination that is potentially fatal for the business. With the key leaders in the room, decisions can be made on the spot to shift resources and focus accountability for addressing the "top risks" that face the organization in more effective ways. This has helped organizations that use this tool to improve their level of preparedness quite significantly.

Hurricanes Katrina and Sandy wrought incredible human and physical damage to two major US cities and their associated businesses and infrastructure. Other natural disasters have occurred in other parts of the world, such that it is appropriate to take a step back and review risk levels and mitigation plans. To help do so, financial firms should utilize tools that can help evaluate the received wisdom regarding so-called *black swan*, once-in-a-lifetime weather events. Given the arrival of two, maybe three such events on US eastern shores in the past decade, the time to do so is long overdue. Scenario planning workshops facilitated with the most senior leaders of the firm and even their partners in government could help our firms to better prepare for such events in the future.

Note

1. Hurricane Sandy (unofficially known as Superstorm Sandy) was the deadliest and most destructive hurricane of the 2012 Atlantic hurricane season, as well as the second-costliest hurricane in US history. It caused tens of billions of dollars in damage, destroyed thousands of homes, left millions without electric service, and caused 72 direct deaths in eight states.

CHAPTER 14

Cybersecurity—The Threat from Outside and Inside the Firewall

It's 9 a.m. Do you know where your data are? As you read the morning newspaper, most likely on a mobile device, you could unwittingly be opening the way for cyber invaders. Maybe it was an email sitting in your inbox that you clicked on, maybe a link to a new business article or journal study. And suddenly the walls of your enterprise are breached—the walls that you have spent billions of dollars to secure with software and services, walls that can be breached in the blink of an eye.

In this chapter, we address two types of cyberthreat: the threat from the outside and the threat from within.

External Cyberthreats

Of late, cybersecurity threats have been a greater concern than ever, including allegations of election hacking from all sides. Although sovereign states are now deploying powerful tools of cyberwarfare, the threat posed by small but well-organized attackers can pose just as much danger to banks.

Malcolm Gladwell, in his book *David and Goliath*, highlighted the somewhat counterintuitive idea that in a clash between a David and a Goliath, the odds are generally stacked against the bigger, more highly favored opponent.[1] Goliath is slow and lumbering, blinkered in his vision and rather hard of hearing. He has also has a rather outdated weapon at his disposal. Like Goliath, the modern large enterprise is slow—slow to react to changes in the business environment. It is also hard of hearing, and updated information from clients and employees may not reach the ears of senior managers who can influence decisions made by the company. Furthermore, a combination of sunken investments and conservative thinking may delay decisions to invest in modern tools. Now contrast that with a small attacking force, the David in this encounter that has but one objective, to bring down the larger one. It dedicates its energies to that one goal and can take full advantage of modern weaponry to do so. This small opponent can change the message and have it understood by all its network members instantly. Today, banks find themselves under siege from organizations dedicated to steal data, individual identities, and account information and disrupt customer services. Vast entities—businesses, organizations, countries—find themselves outmatched by relatively tiny organizations.

It is unusual these days for a week or even a day to go by without publicity of a security breach at a large bank or retailer, and it feels like this game has changed both in terms of the significance and the nature of that risk. The greater significance attached to data security can be seen in two ways. First of all, the publicity surrounding recent data breaches has been richly deserved. There have been massive breaches, and they have upended the assumptions made by customers when they transact in the most basic, everyday ways. Second, in "yesterday's world," the security of a bank's IT network was generally the domain of IT security chiefs. Today, however, it is the CEO who owns it and is publicly responding to it. The issue of today is not just compliance with the regulatory control compliance framework but the loss of real assets, customers, data, and revenue.

The elevation of the significance of data security has been brought about by the revolution in the ways we transact, conduct, and manage business. Customers access their accounts online as a matter of course, often on-the-go via a bewildering array of devices. The same is true of employees. We already take this for granted, but it is a massive change, and it has taken place in the blink of an eye. Large US enterprises, on the other hand, have typically designed their IT security strategies around the paradigm of employees accessing a single IT network from enterprise-compliant computer devices. Although the network was frequently breached by viruses, worms, and the like, such breaches incurred limited damage and created minimal reputational damage. This was because online customer transactions and account data were far less ubiquitous and thus harder for an intruder to locate and steal from. Companies nevertheless started to make bigger investments to shore up their networks. Robust firewalls were erected and virus software was installed. These investments focused on a view of the enterprise as a single network with a centralized command-and-control center. Today, those seeking to infiltrate a company's information assets, customer accounts, sales information, and so on have many potential points of entry from unwitting customers and employees that can easily bypass a central firewall. Focusing on the firewall is rather like focusing on a missile defensive shield when terrorists are leveraging civil airliners. The Goliaths of today need to get a slingshot.

The key to turning the tables in this battle revolves around two key components: data and education. Companies need to go through a process of identifying which of their data and their customers' data are critical to protect. Once identified, analytics should be built around how, when, and who accesses the data. For instance, when does a customer typically access his or her account, from what device, what type of transactions are executed, how much for, and so on. For an employee, the analysis is similar: Which employees touch this customer's account information and to perform which function? Understanding these normative patterns helps identify unusual activity that could indicate a breach has occurred. Investment in tools, people, and processes that can detect deviations from such patterns of behavior is critical if companies are to move from defense to offense on this issue.

Insider Threats

These days, and perhaps it has always been the case, Wall Street needs to worry just as much about the threat posed by insiders, by rogue employees, as from those threatening from outside. Edward Snowden is only the most famous example of this threat: an employee who is inside the firewall and throws stuff—secrets, confidential information—over the wall for all to see. Banks have had their own versions of Snowden to deal with.

Herve Falciani worked for HSBC in Switzerland. Falciani is the person behind the *Lagarde list*, a list of allegedly over 130,000 HSBC clients, many of whom allegedly used the bank to evade taxes and launder money that Falciani leaked to ex-French Minister of Finance Christine Lagarde, the managing director of the International Monetary Fund. Lagarde, in turn, sent the list to governments whose citizens were on the list. Falciani, who worked in IT at HSBC, had managed to download the list of client information and take it with him to France in 2008. In November 2015, Switzerland's federal court sentenced Falcini, in his absence, to five years in prison in respect of charges of "aggravated financial espionage, data theft, and violation of commercial and banking secrecy." Falciani, however, remains beyond the jusrisdiction of the Swiss authorities.

So what did Falciani do that was so wrong? In traditional private banks, customers remain anonymous, accounts are numbered, and only the banker knows the identity of the account holder. Secrecy laws, enacted in certain countries, Switzerland being one of them, require banks to keep information about their clients private and a secret from any prying eyes. Whether or not you agree with these rules, Falciani emphatically broke them, and so provides a very good example of the threat that is posed by all employees. According to a *New Yorker* profile, "Falciani had obtained sixty thousand files relating to tens of thousands of HSBC clients from nearly every country. An HSBC lawyer later described Falciani's crime as "the largest robbery of a bank ever committed in the world."[2]

So who was Falciani, and how do we recognize a threat posed by someone like him? Like Edward Snowden, he worked in IT systems at HSBC and, indeed, his job was to build stronger network security following a scandal involving bankers skimming from client accounts. He had worked in this role for around eight years, and as such was a participant in a number of projects to improve systems and client databases. Like Snowden, Falciani allegedly harbored a sense of injustice, which in this case did not go unreported. According to the *New Yorker* profile, Falciani became aware of fraudulent practices at HSBC and said that "he tried to sound the alarm and was ignored—a claim that the bank disputes."[3] The HSBC incident still haunts Swiss and other private banks today.

Any discussion of global data systems being implemented by a universal bank have to take special account of the Swiss data protection laws and requirements, and this often results in a Swiss instance of the system being created specifically in Switzerland. I know this from bitter experience!

The key to identifying the insider threat and mitigating it is threefold:

1. It is important to recognize that IT employees and IT vendors play a special role in enabling the flow of customer data through the banks' systems and infrastructure and, as such, typically enjoy special access. The controls against them having access to client data and accounts must be robust, with a focus on separation and segregation of duties and withdrawal of access being immediate on completion of project or change management operation.

2. Strict data encryption routines and utilities should be built into any system that transfers and analyzes data so that only authorized users,

those whose job requires them to have access on the front end, are able to read and understand the data.

3. Banks must get to know their employees much better. Managers have a responsibility to know and understand their employees and their motivations.

In addition, modern surveillance technologies can help by reviewing all employee communications against code-of-conduct policies using keyword lexicons and Google-like search tools. Artificial intelligence can enhance this by identifying employees' normal patterns of behavior to identify the anomalies and the exceptions: Which people do they normally connect with, inside and outside the company; what systems do they access, what files do they open and edit? *Know your employees* may not be required under the law, like *know your customer*, but it is clearly just as important and cannot end after the background checks have been completed.

Taking Cybersecurity Controls to the Next Level

A compliance or risk management team within a bank or other company plays the valuable role, among others, of trying to mitigate the gullibility or ethical lapses of the firm's own employees. But actual law enforcement officers take this to the next level. Rather than merely using deceptive measures to strengthen the defenses of potential crime targets, they look for ways to infiltrate criminal groups, pretending to help them in order to stop and arrest them before a crime is carried out.

What if risk and compliance departments were to engage in activities more akin to real-world detectives? Instead of just filling holes in a bank's security safeguards, perhaps they could use some form of espionage to catch employees committing financial crimes or policy violations. This could mean identifying potential or even real criminals inside the company, or simply regulating employees' impulses to commit a legal or ethical lapse. We will review some examples in Chapter 21, where we look at surveillance tools and approaches.

Education of clients and employers continues to be of major importance and is still far from effective. Companies need to invest much more heavily in both data analytics and education on this issue if they are going to stop playing Goliath to the hackers' David.

Notes

1. Malcolm Gladwell, *David and Goliath: Underdogs, Misfits, and the Art of Battling Giants* (New York: Little, Brown and Company, 2013).
2. Patrick Radden Keefe, "The Bank Robber—The Computer Technician Who Exposed a Swiss Bank's Darkest Secrets," *The New Yorker* (May 30, 2016).
3. Ibid.

CHAPTER 15

Turning the Tables on Risk

The survey of the major operational risk categories covered in the preceding chapters is noteworthy for the breadth and depth of their impacts. The losses discussed alone add up to over $60 billion. Table 15-1 provides a summary of the various incidents that occurred in each category. It also highlights the fact that in many cases, a high-profile incident is often followed by one that is very similar in the same category. Very significant losses in credit trading by Genius Traders in 2007 were repeated in 2012; Rogue Traders in 2007; and in late 2011 both sat on the Delta One Desk. Multiple hedge fund managers conducting insider trading in popular company stocks were repeat offenders across multiple years; Madoff's Ponzi scheme was soon followed by Peregrine's; the 2010 Flash Crash was followed by the Knight Capital incident; issues in mortgage underwriting resulted in issues in mortgage foreclosing; and manipulation of credit securities' prices was followed by manipulation of interest rate quotes. Meanwhile, external threats are not going away: hurricanes, tsunamis, volcanic eruptions occur with regularity while cyber security incidents are reported every month.

The general pattern is clear. What to do about it is the key question. In the first half of the book we discussed specific ways and tools to mitigate some of these risks. In the second half, we look at the broader frameworks and tools—cultural, risk, and regulatory—that need to be in place to address these risks in the broader sense. It just might be that financial institutions have more weapons at their disposal to address these risks than they are actually aware of. Trying to put them all together as part of a single coherent strategy is the goal.

Banks and financial institutions have a number of control functions focused on these type of issues: firm risk management, operational risk management, compliance, audit, finance, IT and operations control, legal, and embedded risk management. These functions are buffeted by internal risks on the one

Table 15-1 Repeat Operational Risk Incidents

Category	First Incident	Year	Loss (in US billions)	Repeat Incident	Year	Loss (in US billions)
Genius Trader	Credit trading	2007	Undetermined	Credit trading	2012	$6
Rogue Trader	ETFs	2007	$7	ETFs	2011	$2.3
Price Manipulator	Credit securities	2007	$1.3	LIBOR rates	2009–2010	Multiple
Rogue Computer	Futures algorithm	2010	Undetermined	Equities algorithm	2012	Undetermined
Ponzi Scheme	Hedge funds	2008	Multiple	Futures brokerage	2011	TBD
Insider Trading	Hedge funds	2009	Undetermined	Hedge funds	2010	Undetermined
Mortgage	Underwriting	2006	Multiple	Foreclosure	2011	Multiple
Natural Disaster	Japanese tsunami	2011	Multiple	Hurricane Sandy	2012	Multiple

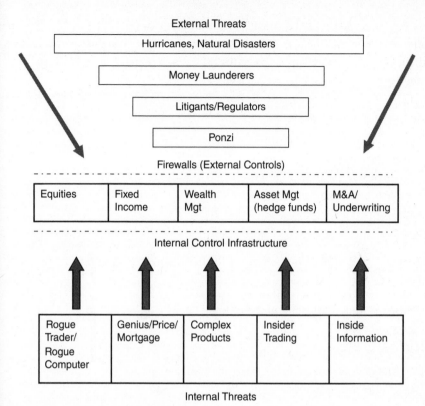

Figure 15-1: Threats—Internal and external

hand and external risks on the other as shown in Figure 15-1. (This is not intended to be comprehensive of all the risks faced by a bank.)

How effectively these groups coordinate their activities has a critical impact on risk management. Each department has its own mandate and area of focus—it's easy to miss the forest for the trees. Equities risk managers may be focused on threats from rogue trading and insider trading, while missing the threat tracked by compliance officers around Ponzi or money-laundering schemes using equity trades to move foreign currency into US dollar accounts. Even within risk management, it is easy to get sucked into silo views of risk. At one investment bank, close to 60 different surveillance activities are being tracked. How are these different activities coordinated and the evidence correlated across these silos?

In the second half of this book, we will focus on overarching strategies and tools necessary to manage big risk more effectively going forward.

We start by looking at firm culture. This is a broad concept, but has a special significance for risk management. Several aspects of culture are worth exploring to identify that a firm has the cultural tools to manage its operational risks effectively:

Building Connections throughout the Firm's Culture

- Seeing the value of your contribution
- Removing silos
- Closing the gap from the top to the bottom
- A shared language
- An open society

The risk management function should not be a separate, cloistered group of cerebral individuals unconnected to the day-to-day reality of the firm that they serve:

Building a Risk Management Function That Is Connected and Interconnected

- Starts with business strategy
- Business is in the business of risk management
- Connecting each risk management function
- Upgrade operational risk

Risk management should adopt a common set of terms and ideas that are widely understood within the firm so that when we talk about risk leadership and subordinates are on the same page:

Building a Common Risk Language

- Common framework
- Risks and control dictionary
- Agreed top risks

Firms should adopt a common set of tools that are consistently adopted across lines of business and function for the analysis and mitigation of risks:

A Common Set of Tools

- Risk and control self-assessment
- Incident analysis
- Scenario analysis

Firms should adopt new tools to better mitigate and prevent risks from taking place:

New Tools at the Leading Edge

- Putting people to better use
- Uses of big data
- Heuristics
- A better operational risk department

Firms should adopt artificial intelligence and cognitive-based tools to pinpoint and prevent emerging threats and risks:

Cognitive Surveillance Tools

- Regulatory change management

Regulations and the Regulators

- Coordination
- Cooperation
- Beyond the letter

CHAPTER 16

Building the Right Culture: Values, Organization, and Culture

Banks lost billions of dollars in operational failures in the last few years. Reducing such losses in the future will come from banks changing the way they think about risk. Too often, people think of risk management that takes place in an obscure and arcane part of the firm. Firms that build a culture where all employees see risk management as part of their job responsibility and make that an integral part of the firm's culture can seize an important source of competitive advantage.

Seeing the Value of Your Contribution

The work of Adam Grant, the youngest tenured professor at Wharton School of Business, was profiled in the *Sunday Times Magazine*. The profile can be summarized in the following sentence: "The greatest untapped source of motivation is service to others; focusing on the contribution of our work to other peoples' lives has the potential to make us more productive than thinking about helping ourselves."[1] It may seem counterintuitive to argue that this is part of future success for investment banks, where as long as anyone can remember, "Greed is good"[2] has been the path to success. However, in its broadest sense, what the statement is talking about rings true: Employees want meaning in their lives, so why not give it to them in the workplace?

Grant's research shows that when workers understand how their work can benefit others, they become more effective. An early piece of Grant's research focused on a university call center raising funds for, amongst other things, university scholarships. Grant brought in a student who had benefited from that fund raising to speak for 10 minutes to the call center workforce about the impact that the scholarship has had on his life. A month after the testimonial, the workers spent 142 percent more time on the phone and bringing in 171 percent more revenue. These results were repeated in subsequent studies obviously tapping into a desire people have to help others.

The steps that many firms have already taken to encourage their employees to give back to society is strong evidence that they recognize this source of employee motivation. It is now part of the normative culture of investment banks to ask employees to give a certain number of work hours to community projects and then keep a table of hours given by line of business/function to tap into the competitive spirit of bank employees. However, giving time and money is still only at the margins of employee activity. There is more that can be done to make employees change the way they perform their core functions. Here are some examples.

Example 1: The Rogue Trader

For this first example, let's think about the chain of events caused by a trader taking risks beyond the trading mandate he has been given by his firm. Let's say he exceeds his risk limits once. Trading firms generally foresee such events occurring and allow for exceptions to mandates or limits to be granted on a temporary basis. So the trader in this case requests a temporary increase in his limit until he can exit the position. The limit is exceeded once again, however, and this leads ultimately to a significant loss for the firm. But because this is a trader has been very successful in the past, the loss, then, may be chalked up to bad luck, unlikely to be repeated. No action is taken against the trader though risk managers at a more junior level have pointed out their concerns to senior management. Six months later, the same trader swings the bat on another trade, again only informing risk managers after the event. This time he manages to make a large profit. Again, no action is taken and the trader reduces the position back within the limit after a three-day period. Three months later, however, the same trader is in action again, and this time makes a huge loss for the firm. As a result, the firm makes a loss for the quarter and the year. As a result people lose their jobs, including folks in operations and risk, who had not been making decisions about these trades.

Example 2: Money Laundering

For the second example, let's think about the chain of events caused by a failure to enforce anti-money-laundering controls. As a result of these failures, drug gangs are able to launder money through the Mexican branch of your bank. With the money they now have, they are able to increase the size of the operation and buy arms for their internal security division. The increasing effectiveness of their operations enables the gang to reduce its price to the middlemen selling the drugs in Manhattan. As a result of the price decrease, drugs become more affordable to a wider range of consumers in the United States, and so usage increases, and with it the problem that it causes.

Fixing the Organization

Taking the lead from Grant's research highlighted in the two previous examples, by educating employees about the implications of their actions, firms can tap into employees' desire to do the right thing, and in these cases to manage risk more effectively. In the case of the risky trades, if colleagues become familiar with the home lives of their colleagues, if traders can become aware that more than just the size of their bonuses is riding on the success of their trades, that there is a whole *inter-connectedness* between traders and the lives of the people who support and manage the control functions, maybe traders would think harder about the risks they take on. Similarly, in the case of money laundering, perhaps by teaching bank employees about the effects of drugs on home life, crime, and the breaking of family and community bonds, they would bring more passion and focus to the task.

Well, that sounds simple enough. Just tell people that what they do will help other people in specific ways—that the people who support the traders day to day in control functions have real lives that are connected to theirs, or that failing to address money laundering can have a real impacts on peoples' lives in the community, and they will do their jobs more effectively. It is not quite that simple, unfortunately. People might be educated into wanting to do the right thing, but still be stymied from doing so unless the organization enables them to do so by creating the communication flows across and up and down the firm.

Effective risk management must also be concerned with organizational design. The next section addresses the organizational barriers that impede the efforts to reduce losses and create a more effective culture.

Breaking Down Organizational Barriers to Change

Remove Silos

The first problem a person with good intentions will be confronted with is the inability to get an accurate picture of current risks across the firm. Management consultants and leaders of firms often talk about the problem of silos, by which they mean business units or information systems narrowly focused and incapable of or unwilling to exchange information with other parts of the business. This is a particularly important issue when one is attempting to confront enterprise risk issues since, by nature, they require an ability to pull information from different parts of the firm.

Example 1: Information sharing across Silos

One example of how important this would be is when a *fat-finger* trade error occurs in one part of the firm—say, institutional equities trading.[3] The equities leadership team and equities risk management, then, do an excellent job of analyzing the system controls that could have prevented such an event from occurring and then puts them in place. Problem solved, and no reoccurrence likely. Unfortunately, the equities group does not share this analysis or mitigating actions with other lines of business. A year later, an incident occurs in wealth management that could have been prevented by putting in place the same controls enacted on the institutional side of the business. So a known flaw was allowed to persist elsewhere in the firm. This type of problem illustrates the difficulties in getting the information that would be helpful to a risk manager or just an employee trying to do the right thing.

So at its most basic it is a problem of people in different lines of business not sharing information with one another. It is also, however, information systems not being designed in ways that can facilitate information sharing. Folks tend to create local information systems to serve their own needs because it is generally quicker and easier to do so. Attempting to build connections between these parochial systems later on is then inherently difficult.

Example 2: Valuation Pricing

Let's consider the valuation of one security traded by different lines of business.[4] Equities may hedge positions with bonds and credit default swaps, as well as interest rate products, yet they may price the security differently than their colleagues in fixed income if they use different systems. Ensuring a common valuation platform and single price is important because of the efficiency benefits and because it reduces the scope for gaming the system. However, despite multiyear projects and major investment to create single pricing contexts across the investment banks, challenges remain. The London Whale incident illustrated this since the CIO and the investment bank at JPMC were pricing the same CDX series IG9 on a different basis at different points in time. This price differential is something that no doubt JPMorgan's counterparties were aware of at the time. Had a system been in place that enforced a single price for every product across the bank, then the change in valuation procedures from midspreads, reported by both the internal and the Senate report, would have been kicked out as an exception.

This type of problem illustrates the difficulties in getting the information that would be helpful to a risk manager or just an employee trying to do the right thing.

Management from a Distance

The second way that organizational structure can stymie effective risk-management activities is the distance of leadership from those they are leading. The challenge for any leader in a globally distributed organization is maintaining a real-time view of activities going on in the group for which you have responsibility. The challenge for the employee is maintaining a relationship that facilitates sharing of information in an open and honest way. The requirement for intercontinental reporting relationships is often unavoidable but there is nothing natural about such relationships and they do not come without risks.

Former JPMorgan CIO Ina Drew was responsible for managing such a global group. Obviously, there were some extremely strong individuals and networks in the London office under her oversight, and in her testimony before the Senate she acknowledged that a number of things were going on that she was not aware of at the time.[5] This illustrates the distance that can exist between a manager on one continent and the team on another. This creates additional risk potentially when a volatile trading portfolio is at stake. There is no silver bullet here. It is simply the case that organizations and managers with global responsibilities must be aware of the issue and build in strong management processes and other compensating mechanisms to address the inherent limitations of the situation.

A Shared Language/No Jargon

The third issue is one of language. The language employed by traders can be hard for folks in control and leadership functions to understand. One of the conclusions of the Senate report into the London Whale incident commenting on a proposal by the London trading team in January 2012 to the JPMorgan Chief Investment Office Risk Committee was that the proposal contained "jargon that even the relevant actors and regulators could not understand." Many times, such jargon simply reflects the way traders speak to one another, similar to the medical terminology that doctors use with one another, or used by other technical professions when communicating with each other. When listening to such a presentation, members of the audience may limit their desire for clarification by a competing desire not to show ignorance. The higher up a person is in the chain of command, the more protective he will tend to be of his all-knowing status. That is a problem, since reticence to ask questions is likely to limit understanding. Limited understanding prevents real involvement in the decision-making process and a greater likelihood to simply let things go, which in turn allows the risk to grow. The language problem is fairly common across all banks—for instance, in new product approval committees[6] and risk committees. Unless a concerted effort is made to avoid it, the language contained in the product proposal and the language and terms that get batted around can quickly reduce the number of people able to take part effectively in the conversation. Firms following best practices try to combat the use of jargon by, for instance, mandating the use of commonly understood terms and language in new product approval or large trade approval meetings. This can save blushes of those who would rather not ask. Such an approach could likely prevent proposals from moving forward without proper discussion and limit setting.

An Open Society

The barriers I've discussed so far—silos, distant reporting relationships, and use of jargon—can all subvert the best of intentions. But unless an organization is committed to open and honest discussion of its flaws and risks up and down the organization, it is to be expected that those barriers will remain in place.

The tone from the top plays a huge part in enabling open and honest discussion to take place. Bridgewater Associates is one example of a firm that takes pride in analysis of things that have gone wrong. Employees in fact are asked, even required, to reflect on mistakes that they make, often in front of a group of other employees. This very much reflects the views of the CEO and founder, Ray Dallio. While it can sound very intense (and often is), the process seems to be very effective in identifying potential weaknesses and fixing them before they can reoccur.[7]

Additionally, a chain of errors can take place, each error magnifying the impact of the prior ones. Imagine, if you will, at the quarterly risk briefing of the CFO wherein the various significant incidents of the quarter are discussed. When asked about one particular incident, the risk manager says, "Oh yes, there must have been about 10 things that went wrong with that one." In response to the CFO's question of whether the problem has been fixed, the risk manager continues, "Well, to be honest, we have not yet had the chance to do a deep dive into all chain of errors and so I can't say for sure." Well, nothing is more likely to alarm the CFO than the idea of 10 things going wrong again, and so naturally he asks for immediate action to address the issue. Traditionally, organizations and risk managers on Wall Street have shied away from holding the candle to such events too closely out of concern that people, particularly leaders, might get the wrong impression and set off unnecessary alarm bells. However, firm leaders—CEOs and CFOs—want to know what is going on because they don't want to end up in the next day's headlines. It stands to reason that organizations open to discussing their flaws are generally much better equipped to deal with operational risk. Imagine the harm where the fact pattern and scenario of a rogue trading incident in one division and region are not shared with other divisions' and regions' risk managers. Could it not more easily reoccur elsewhere within the bank? Effective operational risk management cannot flourish in the closed societies that are so often the case on Wall Street.

A willingness to create an open society, one that takes seriously the flaws and incidents that occur, and discuss them up, down, and across the organization, has to come from the top, the very top. Without the CEO's and CFO's involvement and interest, what happens is inconsistency and differentiation between functions and business units as to the extent they are willing to question and discuss errors and incidents. For example, the head of operations may want every incident documented and discussed in an open forum, while the head of finance may take a very different view. Similarly, one might find similar inconsistency between, say, equities and fixed income. What is needed is a consistently open approach across the entire firm.

An Ethical Culture

Even with an open society and a well-designed organization, it is all for naught if it is not an ethical one. Educating employees about the negative consequences of risk failures, and fixing the organization when they do occur, are a good start but must be underpinned by an ethical culture. An ethical culture is one that demonstrates a clear sense of right and wrong, clearly identifies what is acceptable and what is unacceptable, and that rewards employees for doing the right thing and punishes employees when they fail to do so. Employees must know, for example, that the consequences of bad behaviors will be applied consistently, regardless of seniority and that there are equally, consistently applied rewards for good behavior.

A code of ethics[8] is a good start and an effective training program for that code of ethics is the follow-up needed. The firm's code of ethics should be translated into concrete examples for each employee within the area that he or she works in. What is expected within treasury, equity trading, equity research, and so on is what is expected by every other division. However, it is not just about what is needed to ensure that one stays within the rules; it is also about what employees can do to ensure that colleagues, bosses, and the firm stay within the rules. There should be a pride in ensuring that the firm does the right thing. However, it all starts with employees having a clear sense of what the right thing is. Incentive schemes and employee metrics aligned with risk management should help support this effort.

Notes

1. Adam Grant is Wharton's youngest full professor and top-rated teacher. He is the author of *Give and Take*, a *New York Times* and *Wall Street Journal* best-selling book, one of *Fortune*'s five must-read business books (2013), and a book the *Washington Post* said every leader should read. Malcolm Gladwell recently identified Adam as one of his favorite social science writers, calling his work "brilliant." See *Sunday Times Magazine* (March 31 2013), p. 22.

2. "Greed is good" is a memorable speech by Gordon Gekko from the movie *Wall Street,* which came to symbolize the excess of greed that Wall Street became known for in the 1980s and the Michael Milken junk bond era.

3. Known as "fat finger," traders working in a high-pressure environment will, from time to time, make a simple keystroke error resulting in a financial loss to the firm. A typical event of this type would be a sale of a stock when a buy was the intention, or a trader bought Microsoft stock (MSFT) instead of the Motorola stock (MSI) the client wanted. A real-life example occurred several years ago, according to a confidential source, when a single order was placed in a Treasury auction for 10 billion quantity order instead of 10 million. A fat finger placed additional zeros on the order and in fact the mistaken order was so large that it impacted the perceived level of demand for the US Treasury market on that day. This was not understood by market commentators at the time.

4. Major investment banks tend to have very large fixed income and equity trading operations. These trading operations may have been grown through the acquisition of different smaller specialist banks and so will tend to have different systems for trading and valuing securities. It is not unusual for traders in equities to also trade fixed-income products as hedges, and vice versa. Similarly, entities like the chief investment office (CIO) may use different systems for trading and valuing securities. While moving toward single pricing for each security across business units is an oft-stated goal, in practice it is difficult to achieve. Banks acting as counterparties may work with different business units at the same bank and may notice different prices for the same security being used at a single bank before the bank's internal price departments are aware of it themselves.

5. Reports of the Senate investigation into the London Whale is available at https://www.hsgac.senate.gov/subcommittees/investigations/media/senate-investigations-subcommittee-holds-hearing-and-releases-report-on-jpmorgan-chase-whale-trades

6. Federally regulated banking entities are required to put in place product approval committees and processes to ensure that any new products are launched with the appropriate set of controls in place. Such committees require the participation of major control functions—finance, operations, risk, legal and compliance, trading supervision—to ensure that undue risks are not created in launching new products.

7. Employees at Bridgewater are subjected to analysis sessions involving psychologists and other reviewers when errors are made. This avoids the problem of brushing over mistakes and sets in motion a process to improve processes and procedures to avoid more mistakes in the future.

8. Regulated broker-dealers are required to develop a firm code of ethics and conduct annual training for all employees.

CHAPTER 17

The 360-Degree Risk Management Function

W hile the risk management function still has an important role to play at the vanguard of risk, the firm must organize itself to ensure that it is the overarching business that owns and manages its risks (see Figure 17-1). How effective the firm is in doing so can be a major source of competitive advantage.

Here we look at four changes that investment banks are making to address big risk and ensuring that they have an effective risk architecture in place:

1. Ensure that leadership's business strategy takes account of risks as well as rewards.
2. Break down the barriers between the risk management function and business units.
3. Integrate the various risk management functions.
4. Upgrade the role of operational risk departments.

Tone from the Top: Assess Risks as Well as Goals

Risk Management Strategy

The right tone at the top means that firm management embraces risks as well as goals. For some firms, an understanding of risk is wrapped up in every strategy, every business decision they ever make. Take Berkshire Hathaway as an example. Warren Buffett is known for his long-standing distaste for technology stock.[1] As a consequence, Buffett has long shied away from investing in technology companies and stocks. This is an example of a firm understanding its appetite for risk; there is zero tolerance for the type of risk associated with technology investing at Berkshire Hathaway. While this may make sense for

Figure 17-1: All functions collaborate in identifying and managing risks

Buffett, and we can agree that he has had some success in investing, clearly such a strategy would not make sense for a company like Facebook. In fact, the opposite is true. Facebook cannot afford the risks associated with a failure to embrace the latest technology. That this is true is evidenced by the impact on its stock price from its perceived slowness to build revenues from mobile Internet platforms in mid-2012. Facebook's subsequent focus and success in addressing mobile-based revenue applications have been rewarded in the markets with a resurgence of its stock price.[2]

Firm management should be constantly assessing the businesses within its portfolio to ensure the risks to the business are fully understood and can be effectively managed. After the 2008 Financial Crisis, many business commentators noted the size and complexity of many global banking institutions and queried if they were not too large and complex to manage. Bank of America's growth strategy at the time had led to its acquisition of Countrywide and Merrill Lynch. The costs of those acquisitions in terms of lawsuits with investors and penalties to regulators are still being paid today. Clearly, the risks from those acquisitions at best were poorly understood and at worst were not at all considered. Since that time, many firms have moved aggressively to reduce their business portfolios in line with risks that they feel unable to effectively manage. UBS, Barclays, and the Royal Bank of Scotland are all examples of banks that have drastically reduced their fixed-income trading footprint in the United States over the past several years.[3] Such steps have been rewarded by investors in enthusiasm for their stock.

Risk Appetite

Regulators have started to require firms to make risk assessment as integral to business strategy as the setting of business goals. Going forward, leaders need to be as familiar with *risk appetite statements*—not the easiest term to digest, it must be said—as business objectives. Such statements are a summary of those risks you are prepared to accept in pursuit of your dreams—say, fame and fortune—versus those you are not, because they will likely lead to, say, homelessness or an early death. Let's take a person who wants to become an actor as an example. He may be prepared to wait tables for a year or two in order to achieve that goal. However, he may not be prepared to do so for 10 years, as that may start to clash with other competing goals, such as financial security or starting a family. Take another example—the goal of making a moral contribution to society by performing public service. Such an objective may leave little tolerance for questionable conduct of any type in pursuit of competing objectives. In the Buffett example earlier, as regards technology investment risk, the answer would be zero tolerance, whereas for Facebook, the answer would be closer to 100 percent. However, not all firms would necessarily identify technology risk as being a key category for them. In fact, agreement as to goals and objectives is needed before risk appetite can be defined, since it is the pursuit of business goals that brings risk on their coattails. Take, for example, the objective of growth in Asia or growth of a new business in hedge funds for an investment bank. Both objectives bring with them different risks and the firm should be clear about what those risks are and how far they will tolerate them. The consequences for firms that fail to assess their objectives in relation to the risks and appetite for them can be dire. One has only to look as far as firms such as Bear Stearns, Knight Capital, and Rochdale Securities to see this is true.

Risk appetite can be broken out into different categories: customer, financial, and ethical. We look at each one next.

Customer Risk Appetite

In the case of Bear Stearns, the firm had a strong reputation for protecting and growing its client assets. The objective of growing its asset management arm through innovative products and funds very much reflected that branding. The risk that some funds would fail was accepted as part of that strategy, but the boundaries of that risk acceptance had never been tested until the failure of the High Grade Credit Opportunities fund in 2007. In hindsight, that fund's failure can be seen as the beginning of the end for Bear Stearns.[4] The blow to the company's reputation was decisive and ultimately beyond its risk appetite.

Financial Risk Appetite

The failures of Knight Capital and Rochdale Securities in 2012 breached the financial limits of their respective firms' tolerance. In the case of Knight Capital, its risks should be seen within the context of its objective to be a market leader in electronic market making. The pursuit of this goal requires frequent code upgrade and release into the marketplace. The risk of releasing bugs in the process is one that can't be avoided and probably relatively benign bugs are released quite a lot. However, the release of code with a bug that led to financial damages of over $400 million for the firm was beyond its financial risk tolerance and led to the firm's failure. In the case of Rochdale Securities, similarly, its goal of providing customized brokerage services to a high level of customer satisfaction probably came with acceptance of the risk of a certain level of erroneous trades. The rogue trade in a billion dollars of Apple shares in 2012 was a massive breach of the limits of Rochdale's financial tolerance and capacity.

Ethical Risk Appetite

Charges of insider trading leveled against hedge funds have tested firms' ethical boundaries. Hedge funds are simple organizations with a simple goal: increase client assets through the achievement of stable, index-beating returns. A key risk is the use of what might be deemed to be inside information in pursuit of that goal. There are some gray areas, no doubt, but investors seem to have a strong sense of when the line is crossed between accidental and deliberate use of inside information. Like in poker, people instinctively recoil from cheating. The fate of hedge funds whose central figures have been associated with insider trading has been precipitous and definitive.

Leadership Role in Risk Strategy

Strategy, then, clearly has to be concerned with risks as well as goals. In addition, it would be a mistake to make defining risk statements the provenance of the risk department. Leadership needs to be fully engaged in the process of defining the goals and the risks for the firm and then ensuring those risks cascade into operationally effective statements and monitoring mechanisms and metrics. Again the example of Buffett serves us well. The leader of the firm is generally in the best position to determine the risks to take and those not to take. In fact, that should be a central part of his job description. Do not be put off by the jargon of regulators on risk appetite statements and key risk indicators to outsourcing the thinking on this to risk managers and bureaucrats. These are business decisions, and leaders need to take full responsibility for them. Some examples can help here.

Example 1: Investment Strategy

An investment bank decides to grow its asset management arm by buying a successful hedge fund since hedge funds are where clients want to be. At the same time, the bank has been recently hit by some major scandals and cannot afford any more blows to its reputation. There is a trade-off to be made there between the potential negative reputational impact on the firm by an insider trading scandal or a fund blowup versus the growth of the asset management revenues. This is not just about what the right decision is but who should be involved in making it. Undoubtedly, it is the CEO and CRO of the firm who should be making the decision, not the head of asset management.

Example 2: Product Strategy

A bank's mortgage origination division has found that there is significant demand for interest-only mortgages. These products are generally sold to customers with lower credit ratings and during the mortgage boom included mortgages known as subprime mortgages. After the 2008 Financial Crisis, banks discontinued such mortgages as they had led to the failure of many assets. The CRO and the CEO should both be closely involved in considering any decision to bring back such a product and should ultimately be responsible for the decision. Any decision should consider carefully the risks to the firm, given the history of such products.

The graveyard is full of businesses where leaders failed to act as the lead risk manager for the firm by thinking through all risks that followed the business goals being pursued and then setting boundaries for managing those risks. Arguably, Bear Stearns, Lehman Brothers, Knight Capital, and MF Global all have headstones in this graveyard. To avoid such fates, firm leaders need to be explicit about the risks that can't be tolerated and fully engaged in decision making required to enforce the risk tolerance of the firm. Although it is the CEO's decision to make at the end of the day, if the CEO has been clear about risk appetite, his direct reports should be able to anticipate what the decisions will be and efficiently and effectively manage to that risk mandate. CEOs need to ensure that their business managers throughout the organization and not just their "risk managers" are responsible for managing risk.

Connecting Risk to the Rest of the Firm

Breaking down barriers between the firm and the risk department is really about pushing responsibility for risk management on to the business. The risk management function starts with business leadership and business management and travels down a direct path to the workforce of the firm. Risks need to be managed on the front line of where they occur, not in the risk manager's office after the fact. Employees given the formal title of risk manager are really there to monitor, advise, and, if necessary, adjudicate. While it is the CEO's decision to make, he should turn to the CRO for advice on the risks involved, and this type of relationship should play out at all levels of the firm. Rather than outsourcing "risk decisions" to risk managers, business leaders need to make the risk decisions, likely the most important business decisions they will make, themselves. While there should be accountability within risk for failures, ultimate responsibility for risk lies with business management.

Counterintuitively, firms with strong, independent risk cultures seem to have found themselves with bigger risk problems to deal with. Where the risk department's culture is strong, the job of risk management can become compartmentalized almost exclusively within the risk management silo. In such cases, risk decisions will still be made by the business or the "front office" since any decision to invest or not to invest is effectively a risk decision, whether or not it is made with an explicit consideration of the risks or in consultation with risk management. In such a compartmentalized risk management department, however, the job of risk management then becomes a bureaucratic exercise of looking at incidents and risks after the fact or fulfilling administrative and bureaucratic requirements imposed by regulators. Being relegated to the sidelines as a bureaucratic function is not, however, where risk managers can add most value. Those firms where risk management is embedded and integral to the business, with risk managers available as advisors to the employees and managers who are making business decisions with explicit consideration of the risks involved, will be the most successful in managing their risks.

Three steps are required to ensure that the right people "in the field" are making risk decisions and are adequately informed in doing so: (1) risk management should be part of everyone's formal job description; (2) risk manager job descriptions need to focus on being an advisor to the business and their skill sets need to include teaching about risk management; and (3) risk managers need to be easily accessible to the business. Again some examples are instructive here.

Example 1: Counterparty Risk Decisions

A trader has executed trades with a counterparty that has previously failed to pay its obligations and a bank line of credit had to be tapped as a result. Allegedly, there was a discussion following that prior trade, and the trader was told that any further trades with this counterparty would need to be formally approved by the credit risk department. Such a discussion did not take place, according to the credit risk department, and the credit risk officer wanted to escalate this as an unauthorized trade and a violation of the firm trading policies. In this example, taking such a step would likely lead to disciplinary action against the trader, potentially a firing. Such a step would then incur legal risk since there was no documentation showing the requirement for the trader to get preapproval on the trade. Were such an event to occur, it is up to the business to adjudicate, first, whether there was a breach of policy, and second, what the legal risk is. It would be therefore appropriate to discuss the incident with the key risk officers in the business and make a decision based on their advice and his view of the risk tolerance for the business and the firm. The risk officers should be able to advise the business manager on the definition of trading without an approval policy and its boundary definition and on how to fix the problem going forward. The development of a well-documented procedure specific to this counterparty would be a good idea to avoid ambiguity going forward.

Example 2: Loss Determination Decisions

A structured trade with some customized features was executed. The following day, the value of the trade was written down by a significant amount. However, there was no market activity that led to the markdown; rather, it was due to the fact that the trade was incorrectly valued at the point of sale. Questions then emerged as to where the fault for the loss lay and whether the loss was a true loss to the firm or really was just a mismarking. Again, in such cases it should be the business manager making the decision based on information from the people involved and the risk management department's advice as to what constitutes a loss versus a mismarking. In terms of fixing the issue going forward, the business manager needs to ensure that those valuing these types of deals are familiar with all its aspects and are on the same page as the controllers who will value the deal after it has been executed.

In both examples, the business manager should take the lead in pulling together the people needed to make the appropriate determinations about the losses and how to address the issue going forward. While he does not need to be an expert in risk, he needs to be in constant communication with his risk officers so that they can help him to make the right decisions. To do so, risk has to be part of the manager's job description and risk officers, while retaining independence, need to act as part of the team as educators and advisors to their business counterparts. Traditionally, communication skills have not necessarily been an important aspect to the risk officer's skill set. While there is still a need for the type of quantitative skills that have been traditionally emphasized, communication and team skills should become an increasing part of the job: first, listening skills are necessary to understand the risks as they are being experienced on the ground, and second, to be able to help to craft a practical solution. In the first example, clear and documented communication could have helped avoid the issue in the first place, and in the second example, a skilled questioner and facilitator could have helped draw out the precise chain of events to help the participants understand where things went wrong and what exactly the nature of the loss was.

Such relationships, however, are not built by bringing people together only when things go wrong. Networking opportunities should be frequently sought to develop effective day-to-day working relationships and risk awareness. Some effective tools for developing those relationships include locating risk managers on the trading floor and encouraging meetings off the trading floor between risk managers and the business to review the risk agenda—projects, incidents, assessments, metrics, regulatory updates, and so on. While the business should drive such meetings, risk officers should have the opportunity to contribute to the agenda and to present their point of view so that there is a give-and-take relationship being built from the beginning.

As well as finding barriers between the risk function and the rest of the firm, one also finds barriers between the different risk disciplines and control functions. These also need to be made porous.

Connecting Risk Managers to Each Other

Investment banks generally deal with three main types of risk: credit, market, and operational.[5] To address each type of risks, the departments include risk officers specializing in each type of risk. Risks, however, do not come neatly packaged as operational risk or market risk or credit risk: large significant failures and risks have elements of each mixed together. As long as

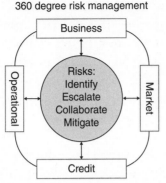

Figure 17-2: All risk functions collaborate closely for best results

firms delegate responsibility for each risk to the different risk departments and maintain the silos between each one, that is how firms will tend to view their risks. But because risks comes in a blended form, all hands are needed working together to combat them (see Figure 17-2).

Clearly, firms that take on market, credit, and operational risks, as investment banks and trading firms do, need risk experts in each area. While each discipline or department has an important part to play individually, it is also crucial to build and maintain the connections between them. Problems like identifying a rogue trader or executing the operational and business requirements of say, hypothetically, the breakup of the euro, are complex and multi-faceted requiring business managers, market risk, credit risk, and operational management to work together. How to bring these folks together can be a challenge in an investment-banking environment where they come from different academic backgrounds and may be viewed with suspicion by one another. Furthermore, each function works to different mandates.

One way to start breaking down these barriers is having market, credit, and operational risk managers working together in risk teams on common projects and risk issues. Teams can be organized business by business, region by region, with team leaders given responsibility for ensuring information sharing takes place and top risks within a portfolio of risks are prioritized effectively. Leadership roles can be shared across all disciplines to ensure that the various disciplines feel equally valued and thus contributions from each are fully encouraged. A formal structure can also be useful where the team leader is termed CRO for a particular business with market, credit, and operational risk coverage officers his or her direct reports. This is a model that has recently been implemented at some of the major banks and the results to date have been encouraging. It ensures a senior person is familiar with each of the key risk areas and can be independent of business management while enjoying its full respect.

Here are some examples of likely topics for cross-discipline risk teams.

Example 1: Addressing the Potential Breakup of the Euro

On occasion, a firm comes face to face with a big potential risk that could significantly damage the firm in ways both expected and unexpected. The breakup of the euro is just such an event with the power to damage currency trading activity, counterparty debts and obligations, market values of positions in certain currencies, operational mechanisms such as trade settlements, trading agreements, and so on. No doubt, the decision of a country to exit would necessitate certain steps by various functions so it would be a useful exercise to brainstorm in advance of the event and create a playbook for such an eventuality. At such an exercise, it would be useful to have all the key risk functions to opine on the various risks that they see and build a consolidated risk framework. A tabletop exercise should also incorporate key business heads and the key control functions. The decision for Great Britain to exit the European Common Market (Brexit) is just such an event and, while it does not impact the euro specifically, has led to many discussions about how banks should address this event.

Example 2: Identifying the Complex Risks

An exercise to identify exposure to complex risks at each business level is another effective way to leverage the skills and talents of the members of the different risk disciplines. Operational, market, and credit risk officers are given the opportunity to identify and present the risks they see to the whole team. The team can then learn more about the risks outside of their particular discipline and can identify the areas of common and greatest risk. If, for instance, structured credit trades were to be identified as an area of increasing risk by all three risk disciplines, a deeper dive would be justified and would follow.

While big risks should be the concern of every risk manager, the operational risk department is more closely associated with these types of risks than the others. What has operational risk been doing, you might ask, to stop all these terrible things from happening? Let's now turn to that subject.

Hooking up the Operational Risk Department

The operational risk department has tended to be responsible for any risks that are not credit or market related. Let's go back to why operational risk departments were established in the first place and what their role in the firm was originally intended to be. There have historically been two drivers behind the establishment of operational risk functions: major operational risk events and the regulators themselves responding to those events. Operational risk management really got started with Nick Leeson and his unchecked trading that led to the collapse of Barings investment bank in 1995.[6] Following this watershed event, the Basel Committee on Banking Supervision, an internationally recognized body by global banks, took action, ultimately introducing a capital charge and a framework for operational risk management under the Basel II accord. Key components of this framework included requirements for banks to report internal events, assess and improve internal controls, and estimate worst-case risk scenarios. Though it has been a decade since Basel II's implementation, there has been no letup, and maybe even an increase, in the flow of large operational risk incidents. While this may be in part due to increased awareness and reporting, it is also clear that a check-the-box approach to meeting the needs of regulators is far from sufficient if banks are to manage their operational risks effectively.

Fast forward to today, and as the costs from operational risk failures have grown and we have looked at some of these events in the first part of the book, it has become increasingly clear that it is unrealistic to expect the operational risk department to prevent and even mitigate these risks. Furthermore, when one sees heads of operational risk still in place after major failures on their watch, the scope of their role becomes clear: to monitor, measure, and ensure Basel II requirements are met. Should operational risk managers be held accountable for operational risk failures? No. Responsibility should lie with the business. This is not, however, a license for operational risk to sit back and watch the business lines make mistake after mistake and then fail to report those mistakes. There are some things, clearly, for which the operational risk department should be held accountable; chief among them is ensuring that the business understands its risks and actively supports the business in assessing, addressing, monitoring, and mitigating those risks.

There are signs that help is on its way. CEOs, after seeing their peers lose their footing at Barclays and UBS due to operational risk events, are getting the message. Boards are demanding to know if their business could suffer in similar ways to peers who have suffered operational risk losses. Both are demanding CROs have greater fluency with operational risk issues. CROs, though primarily still from the market risk discipline, are in turn seeking greater detail and understanding of risk events and risk mitigation plans. They are also seeking more seasoned executives and greater resources for the operational risk function. However, still more is needed to bring operational risk under more effective control.

Operational risk departments have an important role then. They should promote a consistent and comprehensive framework for understanding and monitoring the key operational risk faced by the firm. This is part of their core role, which we will discuss more fully in the next chapter. More than that, however, they can do what they can to promote an open and self-critical culture. First, they can help their firms to learn more about their operational risks internally by ensuring lessons learned from operational risk events are spread across silos. Second, they can help to ensure events that have taken place in other firms are discussed within their own organization and establish whether any pertinent control gaps or exposures exist (Figure 17-3). Finally, they can act as an important independent voice, able to report upward any issue they see without fear of reprisal.

With such a strengthened mandate and operating within an open society, operational risk managers can help stem the flow of these losses and incidents and get some respect on Wall Street. To be fully effective, however,

Figure 17-3: Forums for discussing key risks across key business areas

they need to be more closely integrated with other key risk functions and the business, participating fully in the risk management teams and forums we discussed earlier.

Notes

1. Warren Buffett has often stated his disinclination to invest in technology stocks, encapsulated by his saying: "Our approach is very much profiting from lack of change rather than from change. With Wrigley chewing gum, it's the lack of change that appeals to me. I don't think it is going to be hurt by the Internet. That's the kind of business I like." Companies that leverage technology on an intense basis tend to be more liable to change than others; hence, Buffett's distaste.

2. A week before its IPO, Facebook warned investors that the rapid growth of its mobile apps threatens its long-term financial prospects as users increasingly desert their desktops. This imbalance between activity and revenue was not unlike a routine start-up imbalance between investment and revenue but was pounced on by investors when Facebook was first floated and led to the sharp decline in the initial share price set at the IPO. Two years later, however, Facebook profits tripled in Q1 2014 to $642 million as revenues soared 72 percent, with the company continuing to shift its customers—and advertisers—to its mobile platform. Facebook warned in its first earnings announcements that mobile revenues were the biggest risk for the stock and its stock was punished by the perception that it was slow to capture revenue in this category.

3. European banks cut back on fixed-income trading operations:

   ■ UBS made a decision to cut as many as 10,000 jobs in splitting off and winding down much of its fixed-income trading operations in late 2012.

   ■ Barclays made a decision to cut 19,000 jobs and cut its investment banking operations significantly in April 2014. About 7,000 jobs were cut from the investment bank with fixed-income and commodities operations being most significantly impacted. New CEO Antony Jenkins said there would be no repeat of his decision to increase bonuses by 10 percent when profits had fallen sharply, as he set out his strategy to partly unravel the work of his predecessor Bob Diamond, who had aimed to run a major investment bank.

4. During the week of July 16, 2007, Bear Stearns disclosed that the two subprime hedge funds, once valued at several billion dollars—Bear Stearns High-Grade Structured Credit Fund and the Bear Stearns High-Grade Structured Credit Enhanced Leveraged Fund—had lost nearly all of their value amid a rapid decline in the market for subprime mortgages. The funds were invested in thinly traded collateralized debt obligations (CDOs).

5. Credit risk is the first and probably still largest risk department in most investment banks with responsibility for approving counterparties and borrowers via their credit review processes and establishing credit limits for each. Market risk is probably the second largest specialty with its focus on reviewing and estimating the potential market losses associated with different positions held across the bank and establishing limits to those. Operational risk is the most recent discipline and is charged with identifying and managing the operational risks associated with all activities, systems, and processes across the bank.

6. Nick Leeson's rogue trades, executed in a satellite office in Asia, were credited with causing the collapse of Barings Bank in 1994. Various books have been written on this event, including Stephen Fay's *The Collapse of Barings* and Leeson's own musing on the subject, *Rough Trade*.

CHAPTER 18

What We Talk about When We Talk about Risk

f an organization wants to manage risk effectively, people need to agree about what risks they need to address. Even more, people need to know what they are talking about when they talk about risk. Any discussion of risk should start with an agreed-upon view of what it is the organization does—its business processes—and then what risks arise from those processes and which of these are really causes for concern.

Business Goals

To determine key processes, it is not simply a matter of what the firm is doing now or has been doing in the past; it is also a matter of what it will do in the future. The starting point for risk identification is a comprehensive list of business goals, starting with enterprise goals and then cascading down to goals for each line of the business and its function. Just to reiterate the point discussed in detail in Chapter 17, only when a business has defined its goals can it start to identify the risks that it is likely to incur and plan for those. In addition, goals must be understood so that processes can be built to support those goals. These processes will determine the activities and the operational risks that will be incurred.

Business Process

Once goals have been agreed upon and put into a clear set of statements, they must be linked to business processes. While goals don't need to be comprehensive, business processes do. An organization must learn about everything that it does and everything it wants to do if it is to identify all its risks. For a hedge fund or a high-frequency trading firm, this is relatively simple. For a modern investment bank, however, it is not; in fact, it is very hard—no single person can know everything a large investment bank does or wants or is trying to do, without some help from his friends. Yet it is imperative to gain such self-knowledge in order to manage its risks properly.

This exercise of finding out everything the firm does must be done consistently and comprehensively. Business managers, risk managers, and operations staff all need to be involved in drawing out the picture of the firm and how it operates. When the exercise is finished, a complete picture of all the key business processes should be available to everyone. For an investment cycle, such a picture should include revenue-generating processes such as trade execution across different lines of business, and financial-control processes such as profit and loss reporting, as well as infrastructure-functional processes such as hiring new recruits to the firm. Systems should be linked to processes, and where manual processes are still in place, these should be highlighted.

The importance of identifying a firm's key business processes should not be viewed as an academic or check-the-box exercise. Far from it, in fact; to miss a step, to miss a process is easy to do and can have devastating consequences. In the case of BP and the Deepwater Horizon oil leak, a comprehensive review of business processes would have been extremely helpful. BP had a strong objective of growing revenue through exploitation of under-ocean oil reservoirs. To meet that objective, BP built an effective process for winning the rights to exploiting the Gulf of Mexico resources. In addition, of course, it had to design an effective way to burrow its way under the ocean floor to open the well head and pipe the oil back to the surface where it could be delivered onward. Unfortunately, BP did not seem to have considered, or at least considered fully, the emergency leak capping process that might be required to close the well head again in the case of a leak.[1] That was a gap in its business and risk dictionary. A comprehensive view of business processes should help to avoid such gaps in thinking.

Examples of Business Processes:

On-boarding clients → Executing client business → Transaction reporting
   → Revenue reporting

Risk Dictionary

Once business processes have been identified, they need to be considered for all the risks that they are associated with and compiled into a risk dictionary. A risk dictionary is a common set of risks that everyone in the organization

Table 18-1 Risk Taxonomy

Business Process	Risk Category	Risk	Business Unit
On-boarding customers	External fraud	Money laundering	Asset management
Executing client business	Execution failures	Fat-finger error	Institutional equities
Transaction reporting	System failures	Code release management	Prime brokerage
Revenue reporting	Regulatory risk	Books and records management	Accounting

agrees to be the set of risks that should be addressed and assessed across all business functions. There are two dimensions to risk that need to be considered: the type of risks and their impact (see Table 18-1). The seven Basel categories of operational risk[2] is as good a list as you are going to get of the broad category of the type of top-level risks that banks and other financial institutions face, and the top-level categories should generally parallel them. These seven are: internal fraud, external fraud, execution failures, regulatory and litigation risk, major infrastructure and building damage, people risks, and system failures. Each one of the risks that were surveyed in the first part of the book fall into one of these categories. The impact of different risks should be assessed: financial, reputational, and regulatory (potentially different).

Further than this, risks should comprehensively attach to everything the company does so that there is no gap between the set of risks and the set of business processes that the company has. In this context, a business process can be a part of everyday business functioning or its set of emergency business procedures. The comprehensive set of business processes then should be the starting point to create the set of risks. Again consistency and comprehensiveness are both important. Let's look at a few examples so that the importance of this is clear.

Example 1: Fat-Finger Errors

The risk of trade execution errors is sometimes called *fat-finger error,* particularly, in the equities business. In the fixed-income side of the house, such errors are equally likely to be called, more specifically, *wrong-way trades* or *incorrect-amount trade errors.* Actually these are all the same type of risk—trade execution errors—and should be captured and mitigated as such. When risks get aggregated across the firm for management reporting, if they are named as three different types of risk, then they will be included in any risk analysis as three separate risks. This can have downstream consequences, such as a failure to calculate correctly the cost of this type of risk as well as preventing effective coordination of mitigation strategies across the bank.

Example 2: New Product Approvals

The process of approving new products is called *new product approval* in the institutional trading unit but *review of new products* in investment banking. Although really this is one and the same for both units, the difference in name leads to the inclusion of two separate business processes in the firm-wide process dictionary. The issue leads to twice the number of risks and controls in the dictionary as are really there and may reduce leadership's effective response to the risk.

Example 3: Social Networks

The process of expanding the use of social networks to identify and build client bases is identified as *build social network capabilities* in the wealth management business, but is known as *create Internet-based client networks* in the asset management business. As a result, wealth management and asset management create processes and identify risks separately from one another and list them both separately in the firm-wide dictionary. Again, the lack of consistent terms prevents the most efficient and effective use of resources to identify and manage risk.

Top Risk Identification

Once the risks are established, organizations must figure out which are its top risks so that they can prioritize attention and resources accordingly. The top risks should be those that can have the most significant impact on a firm's operations, finances, or reputation. How top risks are determined will vary from firm to firm, but some ability to scale or prioritize risks is required. Some examples of such scales are listed in the following examples. Incidents can be placed within a matrix, and then that information can be used to forecast future likelihoods in combination with control reviews.

Example 1: Financial Impact

Undoubtedly, the most common way to scale a risk is to use frequency and size of impact. For example, low impact might be a $1 million loss from an operational failure in the next six months, medium impact might be a $50 million loss in the next six months, and high impact might be a $750 million loss in the next six months (see Table 18-2).[3]

Starting from the risk taxonomy and the inventory of, say, the last two years of operational risk incidents, a typical approach to assessing top risks, then, would be to plot the incidence of each incident type against this type of matrix. Table 18-3 would be example of such an approach, where the number refers to the number of events per year.

This analysis would indicate that:

■ More work can be done to identify the cause of the fat-finger/trade execution errors, as they are frequent. While an individual occurrence might

Table 18-2 Financial Risk Impact Method

Frequency	Low Impact	Medium Impact	High Impact
0 to 6 months (Frequent)	<$10 million	$10–100 million	$100–$500 million
6 to 12 months (Sometimes)	<$10 million	$10–100 million	$100–$1,000 million
12 months to 2 years (Occasional)	<$10 million	$10–100 million	$100–$1,000 million

Table 18-3 Financial Risk Impact Assessment

Type	# Low Impact Events	# Medium Impact Events	# High Impact Events
Fat-finger/Trade execution error	70	10	0
Unauthorized trade	1	5	1
External fraud	0	0	2

not be low impact, the high volume of possible events can have a cumulative high impact.

- Significant work is needed to improve controls against unauthorized trading.
- External fraud has a high impact when it occurs, and further analysis should be done to uncover the types of circumstances in which external fraud is taking place.

Example 2: Reputational Impact

It is not always easy to assign a financial impact to a risk. Insider trading is one example of this. Consider the example of a banker at the firm who has been charged with passing on information about an impending deal to a friend who works at a hedge fund. It may be that the controls in the investment bank were fairly good against the passing of such information and the regulators found little cause for concern in the investment bank. Despite this, the bank is now in the media because of an employee who did not follow the rules. How one should scale such a risk is based on the hit to the firm's reputation. Low impact might be where the incident is reported globally but with little blame attached to the firm, medium impact might be where several incidents are reported globally, though again with little blame seemingly attached to the firm, high impact might be global reporting with blame attached to the firm by clients, the public, and regulators and a measurable impact on revenues and client retention. Table 18-4 highlights this type of approach.

Yet the problem with this type of approach is that with the instant news cycle and the use of social media for news, unwanted press attention may not result in any significant impact to the brand unless it is sustained over a period of time and results in damaging impressions left permanently in the mind of loyal consumers (see Table 18-5). Companies at the leading edge in this area

Table 18-4 Reputation Risk Impact Method

Frequency	Low Impact	Medium Impact	High Impact
0–6 months (Frequent)	Local media	National media	Global media
6–12 months (Sometimes)	Local media	National media	Global media
12 months – 2 years (Occasional)	Local media	National media	Global media

Table 18-5 Media Exposure Impact Method

Frequency	Low Impact	Medium Impact	High Impact
0 to 6 months (Frequent)	Negative association with brand	Customers ambivalence about the brand	Customers reject the brand
6 to 12 months (Sometimes)	Negative association with brand	Customers ambivalence about the brand	Customers reject the brand
12 months to 2 years (Occasional)	Negative association with brand	Customers ambivalence about the brand	Customers reject the brand

are looking to measure the impact on customers and only to identify and measure where the press leads to a negative impact on the brand and the way it is perceived by consumers. Such an impact assessment, however, is very hard to do with any precision without careful research on consumer views of the brand over a period of time, something that is normally not the province of operational risk.

Analysis of the same incidents over the past two years at a typical bank might yield a very different set of results than when simple and direct financial impact is taken into account (see Table 18-6).

The impact of trade execution errors is very small in reputational terms because these are to be expected from a busy investment bank. On the other hand, a significant unauthorized trading incident is likely to grab headlines, and the damage to a bank's reputation can be equally significant. This would certainly qualify as a top risk for an investment bank from both a financial and a reputational impact.

Table 18-6 Reputational Impact Assessment

Type	# Low Impact	# Medium Impact	# High Impact
Fat-finger/Trade execution error	0	0	0
Unauthorized trade	0	0	1
External fraud	1	2	0

Control Dictionary

With its objectives, processes, and risks comprehensively and consistently identified and a risk-scaling method in place, the firm is now ready to identify its controls. For each risk, or each key risk depending on the approach, the firm needs to look at what it is doing to prevent or mitigate that risk from occurring. These are called controls[4] and they should be compiled in their own dictionary and be made available to everyone. Controls are generally categorized as either governance, preventative, or mitigating. Governance controls are broad in nature and focused on creating the overarching structures and mechanisms for ensuring that rules are followed and accountability is provided. Preventative controls, as the name suggests, are focused on preventing a risk from occurring. Mitigating controls, also as the name suggests, are focused on reducing the impact of a risk once an incident has taken place.

Example: Controls Against Fat-Finger Errors

- *Governance controls*—Controls would include putting in place a trade oversight function that supervises traders and conducts training.
- *Preventative controls*—A control would include a limit on the size of a trade. This would prevent trades going through where zeros have accidentally been added to an order, transforming it from millions to billions. A second control in this area would be a "second eyes review," which is a person to review all trades before they are executed. Both these controls are focused on risk prevention.
- *Mitigating controls*—Operations might receive a confirmation from the trade counterparty of the size of the trade that was executed before confirming internally that this was in fact the trade that was intended. Such a control is a mitigant because it cannot prevent the trade from happening but it could lead to quick action to trade out of the position if the trader made an error in the transaction.

These different types of controls need to be included for each risk in the control dictionary. In addition, controls should be assigned to an "owner" whose role it is to ensure that the effectiveness of the control is assessed objectively and can identify improvements that can be made. In the case of the governance control, the owner would ideally be the head of trade operations. In the case of the preventative controls, the owner might be the person responsible for the trade system that checks against the order size, while the head of trade

Table 18-7 Control Assessment

Control	Type	Ineffective	Effective
Trade order size cap	Preventative	Trade orders allowed that exceeded the cap	No trader orders allowed that exceeded the cap
Trade confirmations	Mitigating	Trade confirmations not reviewed by trade confirmations team	Trade confirmations led to 5 trades being closed out

confirmations processing would likely own the trade confirmation process. In each case, the control owner should collect metrics to ensure that objective evidence is produced to support self-assessment of the effectiveness of the control (see Table 18-7).

Finally . . .

With the objectives, processes, risks, and controls identified, agreed upon, and placed within a common taxonomy and risk-scaling methodology, the firm now knows what it is talking about when it is talking about risk. Taking the conversation to an even more effective level requires tools and useful data. That is the next stop on our journey.

Notes

1. Following the explosion and sinking of the Deepwater Horizon oil rig, a sea-floor oil gusher flowed for 87 days, until it was capped on July 15, 2010. Various US government agencies estimated the total discharge at 4.9 million barrels (210 million gallons). After several failed solutions were proposed, efforts to contain the flow finally succeeded and the well was declared sealed on September 19, 2010. Some reports indicate the well site continues to leak.

2. The following lists the official Basel II defined event types, with some examples for each category:

    1. Internal fraud—misappropriation of assets, tax evasion, intentional mismarking of positions, bribery

    2. External fraud—theft of information, hacking damage, third-party theft, forgery

3. Employment practices and workplace safety—discrimination, workers' compensation, employee health and safety

4. Clients, products, and business practice—market manipulation, antitrust, improper trade, product defects, fiduciary breaches, account churning

5. Damage to physical assets—natural disasters, terrorism, vandalism

6. Business disruption and systems failures—utility disruptions, software failures, hardware failures

7. Execution, delivery, and process management—data entry errors, accounting errors, failed mandatory reporting, negligent loss of client assets

The Basel II definition of operational risk excludes, for example, strategic risk—the risk of a loss arising from a poor strategic business decision. Other risk terms are seen as potential consequences of operational risk events. For example, reputational risk (damage to an organization through loss of its reputation or standing) can arise as a consequence (or impact) of operational failures—as well as from other events.

3. Most operational risk departments create a risk *impact assessment tool* that assesses both likelihood of an event occurring and the size of the impact when it does.

4. Controls to mitigate risks are generally established and managed by the bank's control departments. The key control departments are: operations, finance, audit, legal, and compliance.

CHAPTER 19

The Future Is Unknowable, the Present Burdensome; Only the Past Can Be Understood

If one wants to change the future, one first has to understand the past. The first task of operational risk is to do so by capturing and analyzing the losses of recent history and the ability of the risk and control infrastructure to address, prevent, and mitigate these losses in the future (see Figure 19-1).

The key tools in the hands of operational risk are internal loss incidents, external losses, risk scenario analysis, and risk and control assessments.[1]

Each element has its own purpose and is typically collected in a relatively siloed fashion. Executing these processes effectively will educate different parts of the firm about its current risks. Those firms able to aggregate the data effectively, however, can create a powerful platform for more forward-looking analysis. Developing such predictive capabilities is where today's CEOs need to be if they are going to turn the tables on risk. Let's look at each of the core components.

Internal Loss Incidents

Internal risk incident capture is the most basic obligation under Basel II requirements (see Table 19-1).[2] The tables discussed in the risk assessment section in the previous chapter could not be created without this basic data collection being performed. The obligation is important for two reasons: first, it is often seen as the most important data point behind the ability to forecast future operational risk losses; second, it enables the firm to learn from its mistakes by ensuring documentation of event causes and control weaknesses.

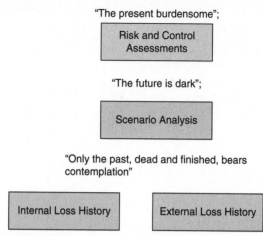

"The present burdensome";

Risk and Control Assessments

"The future is dark";

Scenario Analysis

"Only the past, dead and finished, bears contemplation"

Internal Loss History

External Loss History

Figure 19-1: Understand the past to mitigate the future

Taking the first point, banks are obliged under Basel II to calculate and set aside sufficient capital to ensure that they can fund future losses. Banks develop models to measure what such an amount of capital would be, and past loss incident history is generally the most important input to the model.

There are, in broad terms, three types of losses: small and frequent, large and infrequent, huge and very infrequent. A few examples are provided in Table 19-2 and described as follows.

Example 1: Small and Frequent

A trader sells 1,000 shares when he was supposed to buy them. The loss after he has reversed the trade might be $10,000 or even a bit more on a volatile day, but not much more. Typically, such incidents occur frequently in large trading businesses, especially equity trading and wealth management firms. Counter-intuitively, the documentation of several incidents a day is an indication of a healthy risk and control framework. Typically, little can be done to remediate or prevent a certain amount of these types of incidents from occurring.

Example 2: Large and Infrequent

A structured trade is executed as a buy instead of a sell and the resulting hedging trade is executed the wrong way. By the time the position is sold and corrected, the firm has lost $10 million. Such incidents are more likely to occur in fixed income, where the complexity is greater and single trades can generate

Table 19-1 Incident Capture Systems: Basic Information about Each Incident Is Captured

Incident Description	Date	Risk Category	Business Unit	Loss Amount	Location	Control Failure	Mitigation Required?
Incorrect stock purchased	March 3, 2014	Execution errors	Equity trading	$10,000	New York	N/A	No
Algorithmic trade error	March 12, 2014	Execution errors	High-frequency trading	$1 million	London	Code change control	Yes
Wire payment error	March 15, 2014	External fraud	Trade settlement	$500,000	Mexico	Due diligence	Yes

Table 19-2 Internal Loss Incidents

Incident	Loss Amount	Description	Control	Control Breakdown?	Remediation Required?
Small and frequent: Wrong Way Trade	$10,000	Trader bought shares instead of sold	Sales order/ Trade confirmation	No	No
Large and infrequent: Wrong Way Trade	$10 million	Trader bought long position instead of short	Second eyes review/Trade confirmation	Yes	Yes
Very large and rare: External fraud	$500 million	Sales team lent money to borrower who presented false identity and assets	Due diligence/ Loan document review	Yes	Yes

large losses or gains in a relatively short period of time. For a trade error of this nature to amount to a significant loss requires a significant lapse in controls to have occurred and would warrant a remediation plan to be put in place.

Example 3: Very Large and Rare

Then you have incidents that are larger, rarer, and very hard to predict. Consider a loan made to a person purporting to be from a creditworthy entity and has a certain amount of assets as collateral. In the end, the person is not who he claims to be, either has no assets or no traceable assets, and fails to pay the loan premiums and repay the capital as required under the loan terms. A loss of $500 million is realized. Setting aside capital to cover events large in impact like these is required by the regulators and under Basel supervision.

Daniel Kahneman's work[3] looks at the fallacy of deriving conclusions from too small a sample size. The danger to be avoided is reading too much into a small number of large incidents from a future perspective. The sample size of very large incidents is certainly small and needs to be modeled and weighted appropriately. The real importance attached to large incidents, however, is not as data points in a prediction of future losses but as a rich source of information for risk managers trying to learn how to avoid risk. The future likelihood of a major risk calamity is determined not by naked statistics but by risk management effectiveness: learning from one's own and other people's mistakes. If one fails to learn the lessons behind such events, one is doomed at some point to repeat them. Such information can be used to predict future risk events more effectively, but more analytical tools and honesty are needed to acknowledge where the lessons have not been learned and the exposure still exists.

Despite this, one cannot even begin to imagine the time and resources dedicated to capturing all the losses that occur:

- Capturing all incidents is not a simple exercise.
- Silos and confidentiality requirements between business units can block simple workflow requirements.
- Whether the loss is $10,000 or $10 million, the data requirement is the same. That means the same level of effort is potentially required to capture small losses as large losses.
- Educating people in the business on the importance of capturing incidents is never sufficient.

Often, it is those who are not familiar with the reporting requirements who are most familiar with the incidents that occur. Hence, you may get rogue trading incidents and even large trade execution losses not reported or even discussed internally with operational risk officers. That is why a risk manager worth his salt is always putting his nose in where it is not always wanted, asking questions, sometimes uncomfortable ones. It is not the best way to make friends, but it is the only way to find out what is really going on. An open society will help immensely in this respect.

External Incidents

Risk departments are also asked to collect incidents that occur at peer institutions. This is an important data point to support two pieces of risk analysis: first, to help analyze whether what happened at peer institutions could happen internally; and second, to determine if internal incidents overall are trending higher or lower than at peer institutions. Too often, though, risk departments fulfill the letter of the law by providing reports of the incidents without enquiring further. Sometimes that is fine, but sometimes further work is needed to determine if what just happened at a peer bank could also occur at your institution. A few examples are provided in Table 19-3 and described as follows.

Table 19-3 External Loss Incidents

External Incident	Peer Bank	Loss Amount	Risk Applies Here	Effective Controls?	Mitigation Plan Required?
LIBOR price fixing	Major UK bank	$473 million	Yes	No	Yes
Rogue algorithm	High-frequency trading firm	$300 million	Yes	No	Yes
AML fine	Global investment bank	$1.7 billion	Yes	No	Yes

Example 1: LIBOR Settlement at Peer Fixed Income Trading Firm

Consider a peer bank that has settled with the UK financial regulator for millions of dollars for fixing LIBOR (London Interbank Lending Rates) rates. The CRO has asked the head of operational risk to identify whether this is a risk at their bank and whether or not controls need to be improved to address the risk.

First, the head of operational risk asks a simple question: Is the bank a member of the group of banks that send in the lending rates used to determine the LIBOR rate? If it is not, then the case can be closed, although the CRO may choose to broaden the investigation to any valuation processes potentially open to price fixing. If that happens, interviews should be conducted with the key people responsible for executing the valuation processes to identify any control gaps. A policy that clarifies the guidelines for conducting such work, the sign-off processes, should be rolled out in compliance with regulatory requirements.

Example 2: Rogue Computer Algorithm Incident at Peer Equity Trading Firm

The question must be asked as to whether the bank is in the algorithmic trading business. If the answer is yes, information needs to be gathered quickly as to what happened exactly at the peer institution. Anyone with contacts at the bank should be brought in to understand how the problem occurred and what control weaknesses were at fault. Then interviews should be held with IT and operations regarding any issues or incidents identified in the algorithmic trading area. An action plan should be drawn up for any control weaknesses identified and people made responsible for closing them.

Example 3: AML Fine by Regulators

This is a major incident and requires full engagement with the relevant line of business. Interviews with the bank's chief financial crimes compliance officer identified issues with AML processes and procedures across multiple business lines, including failures to identify all suspicious transactions and risky clients. A thorough review of AML processes and procedures across all lines of business is ordered, and the findings will be shared with regulators.

Apart from the important job of immediate response to an event, external incidents are also important in the scenario-planning component to help participants think through possible worst-case loss scenarios.

Scenario Planning

The third element of the operational risk framework under Basel II is scenario planning (see Table 19-4). This is the most difficult and contentious aspect of the operational risk framework, and approaches vary from firm to firm. Some firms favor a workshop format, bringing key business leaders together to discuss each of the top risks while others conduct a less discursive

Table 19-4 Operational Risk Scenarios

Risk Scenario	Largest External Loss	Largest Internal Loss	Max Loss from Future Event	Frequency
Litigation from underwriting risk	$2 billion	$200 million	$300 million	Every 10 years
External fraud	$1 billion	$50 million	$100 million	Every 5 years
Unauthorized trading	$7 billion	$50 million	$100 million	Every 5 years
Fat-finger error	$1 billion	$2 million	$10 million	Every 5 years

approach. Whatever the approach, the same objective holds: to identify the highest-impact potential loss in each risk category and make an estimate of its potential frequency. The other commonality is the leveraging of business knowledge of the managers of each line of business. The difficulty most regulators have with any of these approaches is generally the lack of evidence for the decisions that are made. Second, it is sometimes hard to avoid coming away with the view that participants have taken a somewhat rosier view of the future than can be justified. Here are some examples of such workshops.

Example 1: Underwriting Business and Risk of Litigation

Your bank is conducting a scenario workshop for the underwriting business. The key risk category has been identified as litigation from shareholders due to losses following a bankruptcy of a security underwritten by the bank.

The operational risk department has put together a list of external and internal incidents that occurred at its and other banks. External incidents reviewed by the group include the Citigroup and JPMorgan settlements with shareholders of Enron and WorldCom of over $2 billion each. They also review the Bank of America Settlement with Merrill Lynch shareholders for over $2 billion. The largest incident identified internally at the bank was a loss of $300 million 10 years ago.

The group, after reviewing these incidents, is asked to estimate the largest potential loss from such an incident at the bank. The group's estimate for a worst-case scenario is $300 million, based on this rationale: first, this bank has a very careful process for determining whether or not to join an underwriting syndicate, hence, Enron and WorldCom both failed to make it through that tough process; second, this bank only underwrites as part of a large syndicate, which has the effect of diversifying the risk from a large single loss.

While both parts of the rationale may sound reasonable, they certainly can't be seen as foolproof measures against a future decision to underwrite an issue that later on turns out to have been much greater risk than appeared to be the case or against a decision to be more closely associated with an issuer than was normal. The issue is that an event that happens every 10 years is not likely to attract a lot of attention to mitigate so is unlikely to drive fundamental change in the way that the risk is managed.

Example 2: Equities Trading and Rogue Trading Risk

Your bank is conducting a scenario workshop for the Equities Trading Business. The key risk category has been identified as internal fraud and potential losses from rogue trading incidents.

The operational risk department has put together a list of external and internal incidents that occurred at their and other banks. Previous external incidents reviewed include the relatively recent rogue trading incidents at UBS and Societe Generale. The original set of internal incidents included in the documentation for the workshop only had two internal incidents, both of which were of far less financial impact, under $50 million, than the external incidents. The workshop group, consisting of leaders of the control and operational functions, after reviewing these incidents is asked to estimate the largest potential loss from such an incident at the bank. The group concludes that the most severe loss that could be reasonably expected would be $100 million, an amount far less than the worst losses at peer banks.

While the worst losses, on a statistical basis taking all banks into consideration, are incredibly rare events, it is hard to prove that they could not occur again. The rationale against such events reoccurring is that a lot of work has been done since those prior events to make the bank safer and that the controls are stronger than they were. Again, however, such a conclusion is hardly foolproof against such an event reoccurring.

It is hard to avoid the conclusion from workshops such as these that the influence of prior internal losses is a very strong influencer of decisions. One can minimize this influence by not including the past in the documentation, but then participants have nothing to guide them. Some banks have begun to experiment with analysis of risk factors to ground the workshops in analytical frameworks that can help the predictive process. This may just be another way of anchoring the discussion, but it may be too much to think one can ever avoid any anchoring bias.[4] Workshops like these can be powerful means by which scenarios can be discussed and avoidance strategies proposed, but they are not necessarily the most efficacious means of measuring the exposure to future losses. Again, the perceived likelihood of a significant event occurring is very infrequent, and so the efficacy of putting in place thoroughgoing mitigation strategies is likely to be questioned without better methods for identifying risk factors.

Risk and Control Assessment

Risk and control assessment is another significant component of most banks' operational risk frameworks, though it is not explicitly required under the Basel II regulations. What is required is for the operational risk framework to take into account *business environmental factors*—in other words, the control effectiveness of the organization. The theory is that once you have the incidents—internal and external—and an assessment of the firm's control environment, then you can make a better stab at assessing the likelihood of risks occurring or reoccurring. The only way really to assess the control environment is by performing risk and control assessments on a regular basis.

The building blocks of the assessment process are the risk and control dictionaries that the firm has developed. Every part of the organization should be assessing a common set of risks and controls. In a large organization, this means the ability to aggregate risks in a way that can highlight areas of common risk and control. Let's consider some examples, illustrated in Table 19-5.

Example 1: Equities Trading—Risk of Anti–Money Laundering

The risk is that the firm is trading on behalf of clients using illicit sources of funds, such as those from drugs or piracy. The inherent risk (i.e., the level of risk assuming the controls are not in place) was assessed as being critical, owing to the high penalties recently imposed on peers for similar infractions and the ethical reputational issues involved. The controls such

Table 19-5 Risk and Control Assessment

Risk	Inherent Risk Assessment	Control	Control Assessment	Residual Risk Assessment
AML—Client moving illicit funds	High	AML detection program	Ineffective	High
KYC—Not knowing client is a mafia member	High	Know Your Client program	Ineffective	High

as AML documentation requirements and fund transfer surveillance were judged as being largely ineffective, and so the residual risk (the level of risk after effectiveness of controls are taken into account) was seen as high.

Example 2: Asset Management—Risk of Not Knowing Your Client

The risk of not knowing your client (KYC) is the same, more or less, as AML, since the KYC regulations are in place to prevent money laundering. In this case, the controls were also judged to be largely ineffective so the residual risk was assessed as high.

The risk dashboard has been designed to escalate risks that are judged to be residually high by more than one business area. Unfortunately the AML risk was not picked up by it, since the two risks were seen as different rather than the same.

The first good practice is to ensure that risks are grouped together under common descriptors and recognized as such. The second good practice is to ensure that a risk measurement matrix (discussed in Chapter 18) is in place and leveraged to ensure consistent ways of measuring risk impact across lines of business and geographies. In the AML example, for instance, high risk might be argued for on the basis of a high likelihood of a large penalty being imposed on the firm for failing to follow AML procedures. The third good practice is to use quantifiable measures as much as possible to determine the risk level: by leveraging the evidence of prior losses and by developing metrics that can provide a quantitative basis for determining control effectiveness. Controls that can be rated on the basis of objective, rather than subjective, bases will lead to more accurate estimates of their effectiveness and, in turn, of the level of residual risk. The fourth good practice is ensuring that high residual risk assessments are followed up with remediation plans to improve controls and prevent the risk from occurring. As has been seen in the recent penalties imposed on banks by regulators in the United States and overseas, there is much still to do in many areas.

While an organization excelling in these areas can certainly collect a lot of useful information and gain some benefits, it will not increase its ability to see around corners or avoid falling into rabbit holes. While it is critical to learn from past mistakes, it is insufficient to prevent them from being repeated. To do so requires us to create some preventive measures and forward-looking analytic capabilities. We will explore this in the next chapter.

Notes

1. Banks using the Advanced Measurement Approach (AMA) for operational risk (OR) measurement are required to include four data elements in their framework: internal loss data, external loss data, scenario analysis, and business environment and internal control factors (BEICFs). The internal business environment includes factors within the organization that impact the approach and success of your operations. The external environment consists of a variety of factors outside your company doors that you typically don't have much control over.

2. Basel II requires banks to invest in systems that can capture and measure the losses from operational risk incidents for the past 10 years. Incidents must be captured and cataloged within the seven Basel risk categories or a similar taxonomy.

3. Daniel Kahneman, *Thinking, Fast and Slow* (New York: Farrar, Straus and Giroux, 2011) writes that insensitivity to sample size is a cognitive bias that occurs when people judge the probability of obtaining a sample statistic without respect to the sample size. For example, in one study, subjects assigned the same probability to the likelihood of obtaining a mean height of above six feet in samples of 10, 100, and 1,000 men. In other words, variation is more likely in smaller samples, but people may not expect this.

4. Anchoring, or focalism, is a cognitive bias that describes the tendency to rely too heavily on the first piece of information offered (the "anchor") when making decisions. During decision making, anchoring occurs when individuals use an initial piece of information to make subsequent judgments. Once an anchor is set, other judgments are made by adjusting away from that anchor, and there is a bias toward interpreting other information around the anchor. For example, the initial price offered for a used car sets the standard for the rest of the negotiations, so that prices lower than the initial price seem more reasonable even if they are still higher than what the car is really worth. Kahneman also discusses this in some detail in *Thinking, Fast and Slow*.

CHAPTER 20

The New Tools of the Trade

For many financial firms, the tyranny of the regulators can be somewhat deadening to the creative juices of risk managers everywhere. As we have seen, although firms have been following Basel requirements for operational risk, there has hardly been a stemming of the tide of losses. If anything, there has been an acceleration in their occurrence.

As we have seen, the tools required under Basel are inadequate, on their own, for both tasks of measuring and managing the risk that financial institutions now carry. In the face of a seemingly unending supply of large losses, CEOs are turning to their risk colleagues with exasperation: Why did you not see this coming? How do I know what's next? In addition to changing the organization to empower all employees to be risk managers, new tools need to be put in their hands so that organizations can avoid rabbit holes and see around corners.

Putting People to Good Use and Avoiding Rabbit Holes

As any good doctor will tell you, prevention is better than a cure. While it is possible to improve the tools available to identify risks, and we will discuss these, would it not be preferable to stop the risk activity from occurring in the first place? Clawbacks and other methods to adjust bonus and pay based on negative surprises are just part of a sea change that is very much needed in the way employees are compensated on Wall Street.

To be successful in reducing operational risk requires behavior change. For years, the assumption has been that the primary way to motivate employees is financially. Research, however, by the school of Positive Psychology, of which Martin Seligman is a key proponent,[1] has shown that there are other paths to happiness that tap into deeper parts of the human psyche and bring higher levels of motivation. Fulfilling employees' drives for leading engaged and interconnected lives will yield better results over the long term. If motivation can be found in ways other than providing a narrow set of financial rewards, then potentially ways can be found to reduce the temptation in employees to cheat.

The human resources model used by banks has, of course, been traditionally focused on rewarding traders and lines of businesses for profitable deal making and trading. There are good reasons for tinkering with this model from a risk management perspective, as we have discussed in prior chapters. However, there are other reasons for changing the emphasis. First, not that such desires can ever really be satisfied, but the gates have been closing on large bonuses due to a combination of shareholder, regulatory pressure, and declining profits. If firms make it just about profitable trading, then traders will most likely leave. Second, how is the performance of those who are not trading or making deals but working in other important functions such as risk and compliance to be measured when they cannot point to a tangible dollar amount in sales or trading profits? Developing a solution to this is critical when their role is increasingly important. Third, based on Seligman's and others' work, there are other ways to more effectively motivate your workforce.

It is worth asking why people still work in these jobs. For many, it is because they are actively engaged in the intellectual effort required to execute their day-to-day work. The happiest and most fulfilled employees, according to Seligman, are identifiable by their level of expertise, years of experience, and ability to focus on work that engages them intellectually. It is also these employees who are the most valuable because their ease with the work is such that they can focus the bulk of their brain power on those problems that present genuine quandaries and judgment calls: the problems that require real thought. Confronted with complex risk issues, a less practiced and less fluent risk manager will spend too much of his thinking time coming to terms with understanding the issue and not enough on addressing it. Understanding this, one would hope that firms would place a premium on experience and expertise in making its decisions about the types of employees to attract and retain. However, it is not always clear that, with the repeated waves of layoffs, firms have been placing a premium on such attributes. With the vanishing of skilled, experienced, and engaged employees, total residual risk probably goes up. Does this help to explain the increase in cost of operational risk incidents in the past few years? Maybe.

It is also true that with the impact of regulation and their requirements, traditional financial firms and investment banks have been unable to keep their employees engaged in the work they want to do, as opposed to bureaucratic tasks they have to do. When considering the reasons for employees leaving banks to join hedge funds, one can't ignore the draw of fewer bureaucratic demands. But banks should still do as much as they can to ensure that job design maximizes employee engagement. Bored employees are risky employees, either because they will take unnecessary risks or, more likely, because they will not be on the lookout for risk.

If employees don't get sufficient fulfillment from engagement with their work, there is still a third source of happiness to tap—that of being part of and contributing to a wider community. Again, building a sense of community is not something that investment banks have done too much of over the years but there are signs that this is changing. Morgan Stanley, for instance, with its 75th anniversary campaign "Morgan Stanley and You," made a concerted effort to strengthen the sense of the community and its history in employees. Other things such as community involvement month, pro bono business planning, employee photography competitions, and charity runs suggest similar efforts. It is not just banks that struggle with this. In a different industry, Yahoo's CEO's call to employees to spend more time in the office is also a tacit recognition of the need for people to have to meet, greet, and work face to face.[2] Banks have a version of this problem, as they have increasingly created physical separation between traders and functions such as financial control and operations. As one hears the complaints of COOs regarding the downgrade in service they receive following such a change, one wonders if the inherent need for interconnectedness can so easily be compensated for by email and telephone contacts, and if this impacts work quality and relationships.

There are many Wall Street employees, tired and battered by recent events as they might be, who still go to work each day fired up and ready to meet new challenges. There are also many who are not, and by taking into account the insights of positive psychology firms could have a positive impact on those employees; first, by de-emphasizing the bonus and money culture; second, by designing work and jobs to engage the intellect of employees; and third, by placing employees within a context of a broad community of like-minded people. Lastly, in thinking through layoffs, leaders of groups need to consider levels of engagement and interconnectedness of employees as factors in determining their decisions. Leaving gaps in knowledge and community is not the best approach in the long term. This is all, of course, without forgetting to remind people of the positive impact of their work on that community and the broader society.

There are other tools firms can leverage to change behavior in a more direct way. First, clawbacks and metrics around compensation could be one effective tool for promoting such a culture in investment banks but require much greater transparency and consistency around their application if they are to become so. Are clawbacks to be applied, for example, for inappropriate or risky behaviors or for trades that in the short term were profitable but in the longer term were not? Will traders be given two or three chances before action is taken by management to activate a clawback? Without a clear message on what is acceptable and what is not, it is unlikely that behaviors will be modified. Also, why not reward employees and their businesses for identifying risks and preventing losses from growing or occurring? Firms that build such metrics into their talent management model will build a solid risk management culture and drive behaviors in the right direction.

Recent research has indicated a growing disparity in income within society generally, and this disparity is also played out within the typical Wall Street firm. People can be told that there are no bonuses to be paid out because the business has not performed but when this is not seen to impact the financial rewards of the most senior executives, that has a noticeably negative impact on employee motivation. Making equity a priority in compensation makes a lot of sense if employee motivation is to be improved.

Putting Data to Good Use

Everyone is talking about the use of big data these days, and so now is a good time to reflect on the potential uses of big data by different industries and policy makers to solve some of their longstanding issues. Here we look at how banks and regulators can use the principles of big data to solve problems like how to identify traders who are taking undue risks or investment salespeople who are fronting a Ponzi scheme.

First, banks should leverage data to expose the objective reality of different traders' performance. Coaches in baseball, memorably portrayed in book and film in Michael Lewis's *Moneyball*, have mined data to expose when long-held views about the value of certain types of players do not coincide with the reality.[3] Mining trade data could similarly be done to challenge views about the value and consistency of different traders. It would be very useful to counteract with actual data the halo effect bestowed on occasion on certain traders for past heroic trading exploits. Such heroism, achieved by successfully taking high levels of risk in a tough market, is often rewarded by supervisors with latitude to take greater risks. In certain cases, such latitude can be disastrous. A disciplined data-driven approach would serve to assess traders' performance on a more objective basis relative, for example, to contextual factors such as amount of risk taken relative to reward, performance of market benchmarks, and volatility of returns over a longer-run period. Such data, by providing a more objective basis for performance assessment, would enable better calibration of pay, risk limits, and trader mandates and would lay bare the reality behind a trader's reputation, which may or may not have been fairly earned. Solid data analysis of ongoing performance should help to separate out myth from reality and help to prevent encouragement of excessive risk taking.

Objective data analysis of the type that might enable managers to identify the truly high and consistent performers is hard to do, however, when the data upon which it is based is bad. How to evaluate the true performance of Lance Armstrong, when we now know he artificially inflated his performance by taking performance enhancing drugs.[4] This takes us to the second use of big data: identifying manipulative or cheating patterns of behavior. Now this is a field of great promise because, underlying many banks' top risks, are patterns of behavior that are hard to detect but that can lead to disaster. Identifying the hallmarks of such patterns would be a major advance. Let's look at three areas: Rogue Traders, insider traders, and fraudulent investment schemes.

The Rogue Trader, of course as has been demonstrated several times, can work at the margins for several years. He typically starts off by taking relatively small unauthorized risks, and generates profits at first that are set aside in a nonactive account to smooth out, through interaccount transfers, emerging as losses in the main trading account. As the losses grow, the trader is forced to put on riskier, larger positions, all unbeknownst to management and supervisors. His patterns of behavior include: certain cash transfers between accounts; trades with certain possibly fictitious counterparties; trades with unusual settlement periods; large numbers of canceled trades; and failure to take vacation. These patterns, however, appear as isolated data points in a sea of daily processed data that includes thousands of other, benign, data points. Developing an ability to draw out the patterns, to connect the dots between these different behaviors, can help filter out the risky behaviors from the benign.

Insider traders work across a network of contacts and activities to execute trades in anticipation of an event that will give rise to a lift or a dent in the stock price. Any types of trades that fall outside the normal domain or expertise of a trader that are executed ahead of a market announcement should be fertile ground for analysis.

Finally, big data could be part of an enhanced tool set to catch the people behind the next Ponzi scheme. The Commodities Futures Trading commissioner, after the failure to identify the fraudster behind the Peregrine Ponzi scheme, has talked about mining the data of futures brokers—this could include patterns of asset transfers, for example—to become more effective in policing segregated customer assets.[5] There are other tools with wide applications and of different origins that can be put into the hands of risk managers, investors, and those who conduct due diligence on traders and investment managers. Analysis of speech patterns by James Pennebaker of Texas University, for example, showed that liars tend to use more upbeat words like "pal" and "friend" but fewer excluding words like "but," except," and "without."[6] Risk factor analysis brings together these different data points to create predictive capabilities, both in the measurement and the management sense.

Can access to this type of knowledge help those who are seeking to identify potential fraudsters and Rogue Traders? Perhaps. These are just three areas that could be advanced for risk management purposes with effective data mining tools and techniques. Will banks and regulators succeed in making such advances, or will we be hearing about the next Madoff, Adoboli, or Iksil in 12 months' time? Only time will tell but it is certainly worth a try. Cognitive technologies provide a whole new class of tools and a new platform to start to make these possibilities a reality. That will be explored further in Chapter 21.

Putting Psychological Insight to Use

Psychology and heuristics can also offer insights that can be helpful in assessing risk events. Errors and failures to escalate to management may at times be a function of various cognitive biases and limitations. By understanding better these intellectual limitations of ourselves and our colleagues, we can find additional ways to manage risk. We will draw on the work of psychologist Daniel Kahneman in considering this question.[7]

First, Kahneman talks about the substitution effect, explaining that "when faced with a difficult question, we often answer an easier one instead, usually without noticing the substitution."[8] From time to time, we are all faced with difficult decisions that may require us to completely rethink the decisions we have made in life or in business or simply to confront uncomfortable realities. It is a human tendency that is worthwhile being acquainted with.

Example 1: Substitution

A risk officer might reasonably ask the question in respect of a losing trade that has gone over the bank's VaR limit: "How can we assess the cause of the breach, and when can it be fixed?" In such a case, it may have been suggested that the VaR model is not correctly measuring the risk. At the same time, there is evidence to suggest that there is a significant issue with the trade and its size. Given that, managers working the issue might choose to answer the difficult question or might choose to answer a different and easier one, "When will the VaR model be fixed?" Focusing on that might allow the convenient notion to take shape in peoples' minds that no action or further discussion is needed until the model is fixed. The easier question, "When will the model be fixed?" is thus substituted for the harder questions. Meanwhile, the breach continues and the loss widens. Whatever questions the improvement of the VaR model could answer, solving the trade problems will not be among them. Daniel Kahneman calls this the *substitution effect*. This is probably an effect that risk managers contend with every day.

Example 2: Anchoring

Anchoring is another significant cognitive bias that Kahneman describes. This is the common human tendency to rely too heavily on the first piece of information offered (the "anchor") when making decisions. During decision making, anchoring occurs when individuals use an initial piece of information to make subsequent judgments. Once an anchor is set, other judgments are made by adjusting away from that anchor, and there is a bias toward interpreting other information around the anchor. For example, the initial price offered for a house sets the standard for the rest of the negotiations, so that prices lower than the initial price seem more reasonable even if they are still higher than what the house is really worth.

The sheer size of the balance sheet of the largest universal banks can anchor CEOs and other leaders in numbers that are of an unhelpfully large magnitude. Could the knowledge that a balance sheet is over $2 trillion in value have an unconscious, or even conscious, effect in minimizing the concern around numbers that are so much smaller? When such large numbers are bandied around, trades with a VaR of less than $100 million may seem relatively trivial and thus make action seem somewhat less urgent to take when such a VaR limit is breached. Could this anchoring potentially (and obviously falsely) cool reactions to the breach of VaR limits with the unfortunate effect of reducing the apparent urgency to act? It is possible.

Example 3: Overestimation of Understanding

Kahneman writes that we "are prone to overestimate how much we understand about the world."[9] Certainly thinking, falsely, that one is in control and has a full understanding of events will tend to limit one's readiness to sound the alarm.

Traders in 2007 had a very exaggerated view of their ability to manage and control events. When the economy was headed toward collapse, many traders were still adding to long positions in the mortgage market. Clearly such traders minimized the risks of the market and the potential for losses to widen should default rates increase. They had an exaggerated view of their understanding of the economy and very little idea of the full extent of the losses they stood to make.

Example 4: Thin Data

People have a propensity to make assumptions about future performance based on thin data. Kahneman's favorite equation is, "Success equals talent and luck; great success equals a little more talent and a lot more luck."[10]

With regard to the performance of traders, when traders have several years of trading performance under their belt, supervisors can begin to feel that it is sufficient to use as the basis for estimating future performance. However, such an eventuality is unlikely. Far more likely is that performance will regress to the mean over time. The part played by luck is generally greater than is allowed for when assessing performance of any player, be it golf or trading.

Having a better sense of the limits of human understanding and cognitive behaviors would certainly be helpful if leaders are to avoid reoccurrence of such incidents as the London Whale and other large-scale losses at the hands of traders.

Now we must turn to a new set of technologies.

Notes

1. Martin Seligman, *Flourish* (New York: Free Press, 2011). Martin Seligman worked with Christopher Peterson to create what they describe as a "positive" counterpart to the Diagnostic and Statistical Manual of Mental Disorders (DSM). While the DSM focuses on what can go wrong, Seligman and Peterson's Character Strengths

and Virtues is designed to look at what can go right. In their research, they looked across cultures and across millennia to attempt to distill a manageable list of virtues that have been highly valued from ancient China and India, through Greece and Rome, to contemporary Western cultures. Their list includes six character strengths: wisdom/knowledge, courage, humanity, justice, temperance, and transcendence. Each strength has three to five subentries; for instance, temperance includes forgiveness, humility, prudence, and self-regulation. One of their key points is that they do not believe that there is a hierarchy for the six virtues; no one is more fundamental than or a precursor to the others. While presenting *Flourish* to the Royal Society of Arts, Seligman articulated an account of the good life, which consisted of five elements under the acronym PERMA:

- ▪ Positive emotion—tunable by writing down, every day at bed time, three things that went well, and why
- ▪ Engagement—tunable by preferentially using one's highest strengths to perform the tasks which one would perform anyway
- ▪ Relationships—tunable, but not in a way that can be explained briefly;
- ▪ Meaning—belonging to and serving something bigger than one's self
- ▪ Accomplishment—determination is known to count for more than IQ.

2. Claire Cain Miller and Catherine Rampell, "Yahoo Orders Home Workers Back to the Office," *New York Times* (February 25, 2013). Yahoo CEO Marissa Meyer moved to abolish its work-at-home policy and ordered everyone to work in the office. A memo explaining the policy change, from the company's human resources department, said face-to-face interaction among employees fosters a more collaborative culture—a hallmark of Google's approach to its business.

3. Michael Lewis, *Moneyball* (New York: W.W. Norton & Company, 2004). In *Moneyball* (also made into a 2011 movie starring Brad Pitt as Billy Beane, a baseball scout who used statistical analysis), Lewis focused on statistical work done in baseball that put the spotlight on long-held beliefs about the best players in the game that did not necessarily reflect reality. One example was the fact that the emphasis and resources devoted to players who could hit home runs distracted from the real sources of success on the field, which came from more consistent but understated batting performers.

4. Greg Botelho and Josh Levs, "'Deeply Flawed' Lance Armstrong Admits Using Performance Enhancing Drugs," CNN (January 17, 2013), http://www.cnn.com/2013/01/17/sport/armstrong-doping/.

5. Timothy Bourgaize Murray, "CFTC's Scott O'Malia says Tech Training Wheels Are Off" *Waters Technology* (February 1, 2013), http://www.waterstechnology.com/sell-side-technology/analysis/2240636/cftcs-omalia-tech-training-wheels-are-off. Murray reported that the CFTC is going to be investing in technology that can help identify fraud through data mining and other analytical methods.

6. James Pennebaker, *The Secret Life of Pronouns: What Our Words Say about Us* (New York: Bloomsbury Press, 2011). Pennebaker is an American social psychologist. He is the Centennial Liberal Arts Professor and Chair of the Department of Psychology at the University of Texas at Austin and a member of the Academy of Distinguished Teachers. His research focuses on the relationship between natural language use, health, and social behavior, most recently "how everyday words can reflect our social and personality processes" (p. 3).

7. Daniel Kahneman, *Thinking, Fast and Slow* (New York: Farrar, Straus and Giroux, 2011). Kahneman, who won a Nobel Prize in Economics, summarizes research that he conducted over decades, often in collaboration with Amos Tversky. *Thinking, Fast and Slow* covers all three phases of his career: his early days working on cognitive bias, his work on prospect theory, and his later work on happiness. The second section of the book offers explanations for why humans struggle to think statistically. It begins by documenting a variety of situations in which we either arrive at binary decisions or fail to precisely associate reasonable probabilities to outcomes. Kahneman explains this phenomenon using the theory of heuristics. Concepts such as anchoring and availability bias are introduced to show how people arrive at incorrect decisions using poor assumptions that stem from these cognitive biases.

8. Ibid., p. 12.

9. Ibid., p. 14.

10. Ibid., p. 176.

CHAPTER 21

Cognitive Technologies

The most forward-looking risk organizations are looking to the new class of IT innovation known as cognitive computing to fast forward their risk management capabilities. Cognitive systems mimic how humans reason and process information.[1] Rather than being explicitly programmed, they learn and reason from their interactions with us and the wider environment.[2] There are a number of related terms that are captured within this category, including machine learning, natural language processing, artificial intelligence, behavioral/sentiment analysis, and voice recognition.

Today, organizations that prioritize innovation can analyze data in more powerful ways to identify emerging risks and new regulatory requirements more quickly and accurately. Those organizations that have outsourced certain repetitive tasks have nurtured a rich risk talent pool to focus on solving difficult analytical questions. They will be able to make the best use of new analytical tools, and be more sophisticated in managing key risk categories such as anti–money laundering, capital market manipulation, insider trading, and potential global market dislocations. In the future, managing these risks with such tools should become more like managing the traffic of a busy city: Jams will surely occur, but they won't lead to major take-downs.

We will review here two use cases for cognitive technologies: trade surveillance and regulatory compliance management. Both of these will be critical to risk and compliance organizations in the future in taking the next step toward proactive risk prevention discussed at the end of the chapter.

Trade Surveillance

As we have discussed in earlier chapters, there was a time when rogue trading was the key risk that banks had to protect themselves and their clients from. It was the original rogue, Nick Leeson, who brought down Baring Capital. Then came everything else: Analysts pushing zombie stocks to clients.

Traders shorting assets being sold to clients. Extreme leverage. Anti–money laundering. Interest rate and FX collusion. Pump-and-dump schemes. Ghost in the machine trades. Algorithms gone wild. Ponzi schemes. External intruders. The list of internal and external threats is seemingly never ending, and we have examined many of them in detail in the prior chapters. Banks have been paying billions out in penalties for past failures. Do bank critics really think banks want to be doing that? Let's get serious. They don't. It is not simply the payment of billions but the loss of client and investor confidence that is the true cost of these poor outcomes. But how to defeat all these attacks coming from all fronts?

One important strategy has been to ramp up internal surveillance programs to identify bad actors through analysis of their trades and internal and external communications. It is no exaggeration to say that proper and appropriate surveillance could have helped to avert or reduce the impact of many of the events that banks have been paying for in the past few years: the LIBOR and the FX scams are the most obvious.

Surveillance tends to be a reactive and passive process. Focus is on past patterns of activity to identify if a breach has occurred. This is, of course, required, but it is not sufficient for surveillance to have maximum impact and unlock the value of the investment. A greater investment in predictive and future-looking capabilities would generate more significant returns by preventing and minimizing adverse events and also by demonstrating a serious intent to create a more reliable business platform for clients and other key stakeholders.

At the heart of modern surveillance systems sits a "cognitive reasoning engine" that enables the analysis of multiple data inputs from multiple data sources. Such a system will look through the millions of messages and trades generated on a daily basis to identify the probability of a set of activities or behaviors being linked to a prohibited scenario. Typically, such systems will share three common characteristics:

1. *Natural language processing techniques are key*. These are techniques pioneered under the IBM Watson Program with its ability to understand colloquial language and idiomatic structures. This is incredibly useful when it comes to surveillance programs because traders and people talk and communicate in idiom and code. The ability to interpret that code will lead to a greater ability to detect wrongdoing. Take the following example of a communication between two traders: "It's raining in Seattle," says Trader 1. "Better take an umbrella," replies the second.

The first phrase is referring to bad results from Amazon. The second refers to the need to close any positions that expose the trader to those bad results. Having the ability to decode such talk is essential to unlocking the thoughts of the traders.

2. *Machine learning capabilities are also core to the new technological capabilities in trade surveillance.* In the previous example, the ability to study and learn from patterns of behavior over time will ensure that the wheat is separated from the chaff—or the good from the bad. In the case of insider trading, a trader's normative communication patterns, word usage, emotion and tone, and even emojis will be studied to identify anomalies. The longer the opportunity to learn from those patterns, the more accurate the identification of anomalies.

3. *Advanced graphing visualization techniques (Figures 21-1 and 21-2) increases the ability to analyze and penetrate deeper into the blur of everyday activities and conversation.* What would before have been lost in the mass of millions of messages can now be understood better and highlighted for further analysis. Graphs can map relationships and connections between employees and customers. The map offers a starting point for further investigation on the basis of factors such

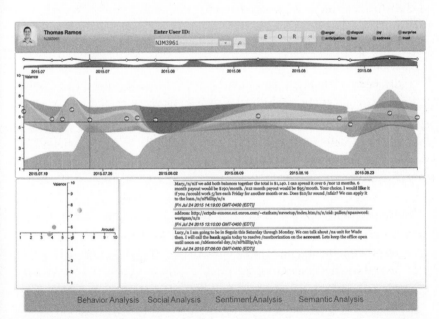

Figure 21-1: Example of trade surveillance visualization analytics—show changes in emotional temperature

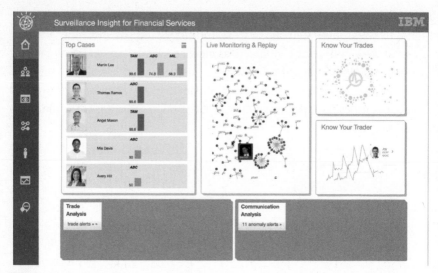

Figure 21-2: Example of visualization techniques to illustrate relationships between employees

as proximity, frequency and intensity of conversation, and potential breaches of confidentiality between people who not should be talking to one another.

Bringing together these various capabilities is what enables a surveillance group to identify bad actors. Take the example of a pump-and-dump scheme that attempts to boost the price of a stock through recommendations based on false or greatly exaggerated statements. The perpetrators of this scheme, who already have an established position in the company's stock, sell their positions after the hype has led to a higher share price. This practice is illegal based on securities law and can lead to heavy fines. A unified surveillance solution considers both trade analysis and communication analysis to flag alerts on traders engaged in this. Using a domain-specific lexicon, the system is able to detect semantics related to pumping a stock through the spread of security-related information in addition to efforts to recruit co-conspirators. The interface then shows the reasoning behind the network of factors leading to an alert for a pump-and-dump violation by combining supporting trade evidence and recruitment evidence through anomalous email communication. All of the capabilities here are required to detect such a scheme.

At the heart of a unified surveillance is a cognitive reasoning engine that enables the system to fuse multiple independent data sources and reason through low-level alerts. Because each threat scenario is fundamentally unique, this reasoning network can be optimized and fine-tuned to include additional data sources or analytics as needed. By utilizing a system that can both "remember" and effectively "reason" through a known violation type, compliance can achieve greater efficiency by reviewing low-level alerts in aggregation and empower better decisions with the use of more data in context.

Regulatory Compliance Management

Today, compliance professionals spend many hours manually reviewing thousands of regulations trying to make sense of the incoming demands and requirements for their businesses asking questions like, "What does this new regulation means for my organization?" The Dodd-Frank law, for instance, encompasses thousands of pages of how best to ensure that it is properly understood, interpreted, and converted into actionable mandates or requirements for the organization. Leveraging a natural language processing tool/AI (artificial intelligence) like IBM's Watson, the legal and compliance team can automate and streamline the parsing of regulations into requirements so that they can achieve a comprehensive view of the mandates that require specific actions to comply with across the organization. The process follows three steps:

1. The AI tool ingests the policy documents and parses the data to identify the requirements with which to comply.
2. The legal and compliance team determines whether to accept or reject the requirements that have been identified by the tool. With each acceptance or rejection, Watson learns and adapts its understanding of what constitutes a regulatory requirement, thus establishing a ground level set of truths about what constitutes a requirement for the organization.
3. Watson applies this learning to new parsing activities and applies it to the linguistic patterns and statistical algorithms it encounters going forward. Over time, Watson's performance improves significantly. The final output is a centralized repository of regulatory requirements that will allow an institution to quickly and efficiently understand its obligations and manage its efforts to ensure global compliance with regulatory mandates and firm best practices.

Maintaining the status quo of applying manual, labor-intensive methods to activities such as surveillance and regulatory compliance are not viable in the long term. Harnessing the power of cognitive tools will significantly reduce compliance costs over the medium term and lead to improved results over the long term.

Taking Proactive Steps

I recently opened a work email with the subject line: "Time to upgrade your computer." I knew that I was due for a replacement laptop and was very relieved to see that someone was taking care of it, at last. But it took only moments for me to realize that I had been caught by our IT security team looking to entrap weak-minded employees susceptible to cyber criminals. This was not a real phishing scam, but a simulated hack designed to prepare me for the real thing. I will not be so quick to open that next suspicious-looking email. A compliance or risk management team within a bank or other company plays the valuable role, among others, of trying to mitigate the gullibility of the firm's own employees. But actual law enforcement officers take this to the next level. Rather than merely using deceptive measures to strengthen the defenses of potential crime targets, they look for ways to infiltrate criminal groups, pretending to help them in order to stop and arrest them before a crime is carried out.

What if risk and compliance departments were to engage in activities more akin to real-world detectives? Instead of just filling holes in a bank's security safeguards, perhaps they could use some form of espionage to catch employees committing financial crimes or policy violations. This could mean nabbing real criminals inside the company, or simply regulating employees' impulses to commit a legal or ethical lapse. Let's consider a few possible examples.

Take a trading-related case. An email directed to an employee promotes a certain stock, promising it is about to take off to previously unknown levels in the next days. The email not only suggests that the employee should invest in the stock but also asks him to promote the stock to his colleagues, promising a commission fee for every person recruited to the scheme.

The employee, without thinking too much about it, talks up the stock in an email sent to a colleague. Perhaps the trader isn't a fraudster at heart, and doesn't even realize that the sent email—meant to promote a share price—effectively violates securities laws. But the exercise has still addressed the trader's susceptibility to a violation. Instead of the trader's email actually going to the colleague, an email comes back from compliance explaining to the trader that it was a simulation, that this would be at best a questionable activity and at worst a criminal act. The employee would receive a warning and have to attend retraining.

Another example would be testing how prone employees are to ethical lapses pertaining to client retrieval. An email goes to employees randomly from a vendor or client promoting a gift of some type—say, two tickets to the musical *Hamilton*. All that is required to secure the tickets is for the employee, who is not tasked with bringing in new clients, to arrange a meeting between the vendor and more senior client-facing managers.

Without thinking, the employee responds, "Yes, please" (it is *Hamilton*, after all), and at that point, instead of two tickets as promised, an email comes back from compliance explaining that this was a potentially serious code-of-conduct violation. The employee similarly receives a warning and is required to attend a retraining program.

These are fairly basic cases. Let's consider something a little more involved. It is widely known that banks conduct employee surveillance programs. In the wake of the FX, LIBOR, and other scandals involving use of chat rooms and the like, these surveillance programs are becoming more rigorous as part of consent orders issued by regulators. More data are being collected from employees, and with more sophisticated tools available, compliance officers are better able to identify potential bad actors.

This potentially gives compliance officers the means to infiltrate networks of collaborators and conspirators, whether intentionally or not, planning to engage in questionable activity—something akin to a corporate FBI. Using technology, surveillance may even potentially be expanded to analyze certain keywords or patterns of behavior in emails and chats, which could reveal, for example, extreme levels of stress from financial pressures or other changes in personal circumstances. Maybe an employee is planning to undertake, or is vulnerable to the suggestion of, certain illegal activities to plump numbers or just to make numbers.

Identifying such individuals would enable compliance to undertake more targeted reeducation and warning programs specifically for at-risk employees. Looking to ensnare employees only so far as being able to educate them and warn them against the pitfalls of committing real financial crimes could be a valuable tool for banks looking to avoid revisiting some of the sins of the past.

Notes

1. Rob High and Bill Rapp, "Transforming the Way Organizations Think with Cognitive Systems," IBM Redbook (December 13, 2012).

2. John. E. Kelly, "Computing, Cognition and the Future of Knowing, How Humans and Machines are Forging a New Age of Understanding IBM" (October 2015), https://www.research.ibm.com/software/IBMResearch/multimedia/Computing_Cognition_WhitePaper.pdf.

CHAPTER 22

The Role of Government and Regulators in Managing Risk

A s we saw as a result of the 2008 Financial Crisis, the government and its regulators play a very significant role as the final line of defense in managing systemic risk. We will look at the role of the key regulators in this chapter: the SEC and CFTC, and the Federal Reserve.

Regulating the Markets: The SEC and the CFTC

The desire to cut off-market, off-exchange deals is ever-present. This was played out in the original battles fought by Washington and the SEC to establish US securities laws in the 1930s.[1] More than 80 years later, the battle is still being fought. Lest we forget, it was, in part, issues in the off-exchange credit markets that helped to create the conditions that led to the market meltdown of 2008. There were no limits to the demand for credit insurance (credit default swaps) and untold billions were written. There were limits, however, to how much could be paid out in the event of actual default. The subsequent bailout of AIG and the complex chain of counterparties behind it was a prime example.[2] The proposal to create a central counterparty, overseen by the Commodities and Futures Trading Commission (CFTC), was conceived in order to address this mismatch and its lack of transparency in derivative, and particularly fixed-income derivative, markets.[3] The SEC, meanwhile, has continued to fight the battle for open and transparent markets in equity trading. Today's threats are posed by dark pools, high-frequency traders, and inside traders.

Second to the SEC in the regulation of US capital markets, and not so well known perhaps, is the CFTC. While the sentencing of the former Peregrine CEO Russell Wasendorf Sr. to 50 years in prison highlighted the importance and challenges of the CFTC's role in protecting customer assets in futures markets, its oversight of the new, centrally cleared derivative market has also been the subject of much critical analysis by market participants. How effectively it can address both issues will be critical in determining its future success.

Opposition to Dodd-Frank was very strong throughout its debate in Congress and continues to this day.[4] Parallels can be drawn to the 1930s and the causes of the Great Depression.

A somewhat similar situation prevailed at that time when, after the Wall Street Crash of 1929, plans were made for legislative reform of the stock market. Most notably the Securities Exchange Act of 1934 increased requirements for transparency. Such changes came under fire from critics who argued that while the crash had driven investors out of the market, the tougher securities' registration rules would help to keep them out. Others, however, argued that the nation was experiencing a "capital strike" by industrialists hoping to force a rollback of the new legislation by refusing to market securities. As a sop to the critics, President Franklin D. Roosevelt appointed Joseph Kennedy (father of future president John F. Kennedy) as the first commissioner of the newly created SEC.[5] The SEC faced the tough job of overseeing the introduction of new regulations while encouraging investors back into the market. Kennedy approached the task on two fronts: He worked with industrialists and financiers to develop more streamlined rules, and he exhorted capital in public venues to return to the market as being in the national interest. Some have argued that, by the spring of 1935, Kennedy succeeded in reviving America's flagging capital markets. Others argue, however, that what brought investors back to the market was the increased transparency and regulatory authority over those, like Kennedy, who had benefited from markets with few rules. The result, nevertheless, ultimately was a golden age of public markets, an uninterrupted expansion of participation and market volume facilitated not by the exhortations of one man but by the consistent application of rules, regulation, and enforcement.

One might well argue that derivative products such as interest rates and credit derivative swaps are at a similar turning point now as equities were in 1935. While there will be some costs borne by some in the short term, all will arguably benefit in the long term from the greater transparency afforded by the planned changes. Over time, the trust in fair and efficient market functioning afforded by greater transparency will ensure increased liquidity and market participation. In addition, a process by which collateral will have to be put up in respect of positions taken and reported will provide an additional cushion to the market and should act to discourage excessive speculative position taking. The additional reporting of positions will ensure that regulators and market participants have a better handle on the levels of risk and liquidity in the market. The question, though, is whether the CFTC will be able to act effectively when they do have that data. There are those who argue, for instance, that regulators knew how much risk was being taken in the London Whale case, but that did not help them to take appropriate action. At what point in the risk does it become truly actionable?

This gets us back to the advantage potentially provided by big data. If the CFTC is able to build capabilities to analyze the data it has—for investigation of growing risk levels in an AIG-like scenario, for potential fraud in a Peregrine scenario, or a shortfall of customer assets in an MF Global scenario—then it could start to add real value as a risk manager as well as an regulatory enforcer.

One question, however, that has been popularly posed is whether the CFTC has the wherewithal and the leadership in place, like Joe Kennedy in 1934, to oversee such a transition to a transparent market place. It is clear, for example, from the recent MF Global and Peregrine episodes, that the CFTC is challenged even in its ability to execute on its existing responsibilities. There are, however, three lessons to be taken from the experience of 1935 that should provide some crumbs of comfort to such doubters:

1. If one can provide clear, focused, and unwavering leadership, great obstacles can be overcome, like, for example, the opposition of those entrenched in the old ways of doing things.

2. If regulators/the CFTC can provide a set of clear rules and apply them consistently to all key players, the winners will be those able to take advantage of the new economic opportunities afforded by the new ways of doing things.

3. New technologies will be developed to facilitate the new ways of doing things better, faster, and with greater transparency, which will quickly make the old forms of deal sheets and bilateral negotiations seem outdated and inefficient. This can be seen in the rapid development of technologies from the 1930s to the present day to support faster trade execution and better pricing information. The almost daily announcements of new technology solutions to execute on the new rules for swaps appear to support this argument.

While the derivative products subject to the new clearing rules may be more complex than the cash equity products regulated in the 1930s, the leap forward is not one of the imagination, as it once was. Market participants understand how to operate in a transparent marketplace. All that the CFTC has to do is provide unwavering determination, a clear set of rules, and a regulatory environment that encourages technological innovation. Easy, right?

So let's turn to those equity markets where folks have recently grown more concerned about the prospect of unfair and nontransparent markets. To summarize these concerns:

- There are trades disappearing into dark pools.
- Some traders are benefiting from greater speed to execute trades, with an effective price advantage over their slower competitors.
- There is fear that the whole thing is rigged in favor of those with access to insider information.

Addressing these concerns and risks is really the province of that other regulator, the SEC. The SEC, of course, is the perennial punching bag for critics of regulators' incompetence and has been blamed for such events as Enron, Madoff, and the 1990s Internet Bubble. The decision in 2013 to appoint Mary Joe White, an ex-United States Attorney for the Southern District of Manhattan, as chair of the SEC sent a strong signal to the markets and US investors.

Since White came to the role at the SEC, she signaled a readiness to take on the world of high frequency trading, dark pools, and other financial bad acts. This directive was given further impetus by the press and discussion generated by Michael Lewis's book *Flash Boys*.[6] White and the SEC signaled their readiness to address the issue with a raft of proposals. With White's recent departure from the SEC, following the recent presidential election, it is yet to be seen whether this strong hand in regulating the markets will be continued.

Regulating Risk Taking: The Federal Reserve and the Treasury

Much discussion followed the bailout of Bear Stearns as to whether or not the readiness for the federal government to step in to rescue large institutions was encouraging risk taking. What followed was a zigzag course resulting in the decision to allow Lehman Brothers to fail but then to bail out AIG. Whatever the rights and wrongs of these decisions, it is clear that risk taking and traders thinking on a daily basis was significantly impacted. Another decision made by the Treasury to intervene in the secondary debt markets to provide liquidity likely had an even more significant impact on risk taking. Indeed, the most significant impact, the largest negative swings in daily market movement in the years after the 2008 Financial Crisis, followed remarks from Fed Chairman Ben Bernanke indicating a deceleration of the Treasury's debt purchase program. The purchases provided major liquidity and support to the markets. While the objective of maintaining low levels of interest rates was achieved, risk taking in equity markets was encouraged.

A second feature of the Federal Reserve has been increased transparency provided to the markets to its thinking, plans, and forward strategy.[7] Additional transparency was believed to be a good thing in that it was expected to facilitate greater stability in the markets. Others take the view, however, that by providing greater certainty to traders, the Federal Reserve has actually, on the contrary, helped to destabilize markets.[8] The thinking goes that, by providing greater certainty, traders are encouraged to take more risks. What is more helpful is actually providing sudden surprises that cannot be anticipated by traders and, hence, more circumspection is required in trading strategies. The research undertaken by of the University of Cambridge identified patterns that indicated that greater volatility followed Fed announcements. Whatever is the case, it is clear that the Federal Reserve has a major impact on risk management in the markets.

Regulatory Reform since the 2008 Financial Crisis

Wall Street hawks hungry for more aggressive reforms following the crisis should avoid letting the perfect be the enemy of the good.

What do I mean? Toward the end of the just-released movie *The Big Short* the narrator recites a list of post-crisis developments—sure to be the wish list of any industry critic—that in fact haven't happened. They include the arrests of multiple leading players involved in the 2008 meltdown, and a breakup of the biggest banks. Indeed outspoken progressives seem to give flunking grades to the industry's post-crisis response efforts as they push for more drastic reforms. But focusing too heavily on what has not happened ignores the positive changes in industry practices that have taken place since the crisis. It is worthwhile to summarize them.

More Cautious Traders

First, there has been a cultural shift at the major banks away from short-term risk-taking. Examples of this include the fact that traders' trading limits are managed more carefully and comprehensively by market risk officers. Firms have also reduced incentives for traders to take long-term risks for short-term gains. Bonus payments are held back or other punitive actions are taken when traders have been found to have exceeded their trading limits or gone outside of their trading mandate.

Since the *Big Short* era, a more aggressive risk officer has come to the fore, one who has a seat at the table when new trades are being discussed. The risk officer's opinion is treated more seriously by trading operations executives operating under the assumption that that short-term gain is not the only factor in deciding whether to move forward with a trade. Furthermore, officers focused on risk modeling have put in place important industry strength controls that have been able to provide more transparency around new trades, model changes, and complex trading activities.

In fact, perhaps the clearest sign of a shift away from risky trading is that more than a few traders—complaining of bureaucracy and compliance overreach—have left to go to work for hedge funds, organizations perhaps more perfectly designed to take on extreme trading risks.

Regulations with Actual Bite

Second, regulatory changes have begun to have a noticeably positive effect. The Basel III regime has led to significant deleveraging by US and European banks and this has taken some important elements of high risk out of the equation. Regulators have a much better view into the liquidity positions of their regulated entities through the Federal Reserve's Comprehensive Capital Analysis and Review and other stress test measures, deploying their own conservative models into the risk assessment process.

Significant new disciplines around data management and data governance driven by Dodd-Frank Act requirements point to a greater certainty and understanding of a bank's true positions and risk exposures. The Volcker Rule is having a clearly visible impact. The role of investment banks in trading capital has been reduced. Banks that had aggressively invested in hedge funds and proprietary trading desks have closed down those desks, restricting all prop trading activity. Swap transactions that used to take place only bilaterally—a risky proposition that had disastrous effects in the crisis—are now moving to exchanges as required by the 2010 reform law.

A Shift Toward Advisory Services

Third, the business strategy of leading investment banks has changed. One good example is Morgan Stanley, which for several years now has explicitly focused on increasing the proportion of its revenues from stable sources, most particularly wealth management and institutional trading services. This strategy has borne fruit, exemplified by the successful integration of Smith Barney, of which Morgan Stanley purchased a majority stake from Citigroup.

A more prudent strategy is also demonstrated by increased revenue from commission-based trading activity; the level of capital assigned to profit-making from complex trading activity has been reduced. This was reinforced by the organizational announcements made in the last week.

The narrator in *The Big Short* was not too optimistic for the future and our ability to prevent a reoccurrence of the events of 2008. But the changes I have outlined above represent a pretty good defense against a repeat of the financial crisis.

Sure, a different scenario could emerge to trigger a future crisis. One concern often expressed in the post-Dodd-Frank era is that the huge emphasis on decisions needing documentation, verification, and validation from multiple control layers is diverting too much time and resources away from actual risk management and professional judgment. Ideally, banks and regulators can find the appropriate balance of risk management and business innovation to limit the likelihood or effects of such a scenario going forward.

At time of writing, there are now questions being raised as to whether or not these reforms will remain in place. Watch this space to see if progress towards reducing risk from another Financial Crisis continues or recedes.

Notes

1. The Securities and Exchange Commission was established under the 1934 Securities Exchange Act. After the crash of 1929 that led to the Great Depression, the Act was established to promote greater transparency in the equity markets.

2. AIG's cash squeeze was driven in large part by losses in a unit separate from its traditional insurance businesses. That financial products unit, which has been a part of AIG for years, sold the credit default swap contracts designed to protect investors against default in an array of assets, including subprime mortgages. But as the housing market crumbled, the value of those contracts dropped sharply, driving $18 billion in losses over three quarters and forcing AIG to put up billions of dollars in collateral. AIG raised $20 billion earlier in 2008. But the ongoing demands strained the holding company's resources. These moves ultimately forced the US

government in September 2008 to seize control of AIG—one of the world's biggest insurers—in an $85 billion deal that signaled the intensity of its concerns about the danger a collapse could pose to the financial system.

3. The proposal and implementation of a central counterparty for the creation of an open and transparent exchange for swaps was introduced to counter the over-the-counter market and reduce the risk posed by the inability to keep track of all the transactions undertaken via the by-party mechanism. The by-party mechanism was held up as a primary cause of the imbalance in risk taken in underwriting credit risks that far outweighed the ability to pay out in the event of a credit event.

4. Financial services lobbyists were defeated in December 2012 after a federal judge sided with regulators who wanted to keep a closer eye on freewheeling derivatives trading. In a 93-page ruling, Judge Beryl Howell dismissed a lawsuit filed by financial industry groups against the CFTC. In their suit, the groups, led by the US Chamber of Commerce and the Investment Company Institute, challenged a rule that forced mutual funds and other investment companies to register with the commission. Judge Howell noted that the 2008 financial crisis was "due in significant part to derivatives trading, lack of transparency, and the lack of regulatory oversight, all of which prompted enactment of Dodd-Frank." https://dealbook.nytimes.com/2012/12/12/in-a-victory-for-regulators-judge-dismisses-a-mutual-fund-lawsuit/.

5. Far from being a proponent of fair and transparent markets, Joseph Kennedy was widely seen as someone who had benefited from their opposite—opaque and monopoly competition.

6. Michael Lewis, *Flash Boys* (New York: W. W. Norton & Company, 2014), provoked much controversy regarding its discussion of the activities and tactics of high-frequency trading firms. Regardless of the rights and wrongs of the allegations, the SEC has signaled its intent to address these concerns to ensure that markets continue to be fair and accessible on an equitable basis by all market players.

7. Former Fed chairman Ben Bernanke was determined to continue the process initiated by his predecessor, Alan Greenspan, to provide greater transparency to the deliberations and strategy of the Federal Reserve. The minutes of the monthly meetings are publicly available.

8. John Coates, "The Biology of Risk," *New York Times Sunday Review*, June 7, 2014, argues that policy uncertainty can help to target risk taking and prevent sustained and unwanted over exuberance.

CHAPTER 23

Case Studies and Guiding Principles in Planning for Disaster

Given the track record in recent years of risk management in preparing for and addressing emerging big risks, it is clear that this is a weaker part of firms' risk management capabilities. How can we better plan for future risk events? In boardrooms and discussions with their chief risk officers, leaders of firms desperately want to know: What should we be worrying about, what is the next thing that is going to blow us up?

A look at major disasters in history: one wrought by God (the biblical flood) and two by man (Hitler's 1940 invasion of France and the 1967 Six-Day War in Gaza) can provide us with some guiding principles on planning for such events.

First Guiding Principle: Develop Multiple Scenarios and Optionality

Consider the various risk scenarios that require plans to be drawn up to address. In the example of the biblical flood (described in the book of Genesis, chapters 6 to 9), Noah knew exactly how and when the impending catastrophe would unfold. In the complex world of today that is unusual to say the least. There are usually several unknown elements—for example, when an event will take place and how exactly it will manifest.

An interesting case in history is the German invasion of France in the Second World War. France was fearful of a resurgent Germany ever since the harsh terms of the Treaty of Versailles had been imposed on Germany after its defeat in the First World War.[1] The French military planners in the 1930s, expecting an attack, constructed the infamous Maginot Line along its border with Germany as their line of defense. French planners, however, did not want to wall off Belgium and probably did not invest sufficient time in considering the many different ways an attack could come. Instead, they jumped straight to a single solution. Good risk managers tend to devote as much time up front to weighing and deliberating over the various ways an event could manifest itself as to developing solutions to address them. In addition, the likelihood of different scenarios may change and so it is important to constantly revisit and recalibrate each of the key risk scenarios as well as identify new ones if justified by events and information.

In contrast to the France example prior to World War II, the modern state of Israel plans for multiple specific scenarios and always has done so. Surrounded by multiple enemies across all of its borders, Israel has very shallow defense possibilities. The country is geographically very small and so has always been vulnerable to a surprise invasion from a conventional army. Dangerous risk scenarios conceived from the start of its existence included simultaneous attacks from its borders with Egypt, Jordan, and Syria. Such scenarios have in the past two decades been added to unconventional attacks such as suicide bombers and missiles launched at civilian settlements and cities. Nuclear attack from Iran is the latest scenario to be included in Israeli planners' thinking. These are all serious scenarios and highlight the point that risk managers don't necessarily have the luxury to choose which one or two scenarios to prepare for; more often than not, one has to prepare for all of them.[2]

Second Guiding Principle: Develop Strategies to Match the Scenarios

Noah receives top marks for designing and executing a strategy, albeit with divine assistance, perfectly suited to the scenario he expected. His strategy design was based on the rational conclusion that neither prevention of the upcoming disaster nor saving any of the existing environment were reasonable options and that a mitigation strategy, limited to saving his family (and mankind potentially) and the entire animal kingdom, was all he could reasonably achieve. The ark was perfectly suited to that purpose. The allocation of resources—it did take a hundred years of his life—was well matched to the required investment and potential outcome.

In the case of the Maginot Line, the outcome was not so successful. While the Maginot did successfully prevent a direct attack on France, it ultimately failed since the German army invaded Holland and then Belgium before moving into France. In addition, the almost exclusive allocation of French military spending to the perfection of the Maginot Line defense network resulted in inadequate resourcing of other aspects of France's military infrastructure and strategy. In particular, the new mobile armored vehicles on land and in the air that enabled the German Army to move so quickly through the Low Countries were not matched by French investments in similar hardware. The decisive strike by the German army took them to Paris within the space of five days and enabled them to cut off the main French forces at Maginot and force a quick surrender.

In defense of the French planners, the decision to build the Maginot Line had popular support, and Belgium's neutrality status would not have been considered so lightly violated by the German Army. The critical failure, these factors notwithstanding, was that of neglecting to develop other controls and strategies to contend with an attack other than one on land directly from Germany.

In contrast, having identified the various scenarios, Israel has developed strategies to meet each one. Many of these strategies have required resources and execution capabilities. Most recently, Israel invested in a multiyear program to develop missile defense capabilities, known as the Iron Dome Defense Shield. This strategy appears to have been well suited to the mid-range missile attack scenario that was directed against it from Gaza in 2012. Official Israel statements in November 2012 indicated that Iron Dome had intercepted 400+ rockets leading one defense reporter at least to write that "the lack of Israeli casualties suggests Iron Dome is the most effective, most-tested missile shield the world has ever seen."[3]

Third Guiding Principle: Understand How the World Is Changing

If one is to prepare adequately for future and emerging risks, one has to mine information and intelligence to ensure that the assumptions behind scenarios and strategies continue to make sense. Noah's information was perfect, of course, and highlighted the continued relevance of his strategy—people were not changing (or at least God's view of them), and so God remained determined to send the flood. In the case of France, intelligence on Hitler's precise intentions was not available to French military planners, who anyway did not necessarily take the new Chancellor (Hitler) at his word. Their belief that a German attack would be launched directly across the Rhine via Alsace and Lorraine did not change, and as a result, their investment francs continued to pour into the Maginot defensive line. There was, however, plenty of data for them to mine. First of all, it was clear from Hitler's actions in Eastern Europe and Sudetenland that he did not respect treaties and sovereignty.[4] Second, there was much data to show that Germany was investing heavily in mobile armor, planes included, that could enable German forces to rapidly bypass defensive lines. The conclusion that the next war would be fought using different tools and strategies was drawn by at least one of the allies, Great Britain. Britain responded, albeit late, with a similar investment program in mobile resources. French military planners, on the other hand, either did not have data, or if they did, failed to leverage the data in a way that would have allowed them to reevaluate the efficacy of their strategies.

Fourth Guiding Principle: Build Political Will to Resource the Chosen Strategy

Noah failed to build a popular mandate, but his strategy did not require one. In general, however, this is critical. It is unlikely that the French populace would have supported anything other than its chosen "hide behind a wall" strategy, but in any case, French leaders did not seek to convince its people of any alternative.

It is not necessarily the populace that needs convincing in these cases. Israeli military planners, for example, do not need to convince their own population.

Rather, it is its key allies that it must work to convince, most especially the United States. Most of the time, the Israelis have been successful in convincing the United States to support its projects. In the case of the Iron Dome, for instance, Israel could not have been successful in its development without the Obama administration's agreement to help fund it and provide vital technical expertise.

The examples discussed here are simply illustrations of the potential danger posed by different risk scenarios. Whatever the specific issue, however, firms need to develop capabilities to peer into the future and think creatively about the risks it may bring and the possible solutions to mitigate those same risks. It is all too easy to focus on the day-to-day issues and miss the big risks that are just beyond. There are four steps to avoiding that error:

1. Detail the different scenarios.
2. Design strategies appropriate to these scenarios.
3. Objectively assess the data.
4. Build the political will to undertake the strategies identified.

The fourth step, of course, is the most difficult, and it should start with building a consensus among key decision makers around future scenarios and what strategies make most sense to meet them.

Notes

1. For a treatment of the Treaty of Versailles, subsequent building of the Maginot Line, and its striking failure to mitigate Hitler's invasion, A. J. P. Taylor, *Origins of the Second World War* (Robbinsdale, MN: Fawcett Books, 1961) remains the classic.
2. Various works by military historians have described effectively Israel's military struggles and the necessity of its defense strategies. See, for example, Ian Bickerton and Carla Klausner, *A History of the Arab-Israeli Conflict* (Englewood Cliffs, NJ: Pearson Education, 1991/2009).
3. Mark Thompson, "Iron Dome: A Missile Shield that Works," *Time* (November 19, 2012).
4. Hitler proved adept at making and unmaking treaties as he pleased. This is well documented. For a thorough discussion, Alan Bullock, *Hitler: A Study in Tyranny* (New York: Harper Collins, 1959), is still worth reading.

CHAPTER 24

The Risk Management Society and Its Friends

As we have just seen, every kind of society needs to manage its risks effectively, whether it is a small or large firm, a city, a state, or a country. I have also made the case that risk management is ideally not a separate function but is sewn into the very fabric of society such that ordinary employees or citizens become managers of risk. Fighting terrorism on the home front, for example, can only be effective when citizens are aware of the dangers and are educated to identify the potential threat behind, for example, an ownerless bag left on a train. For a society to function effectively in this way, several attributes need to be present. Here, we will look at these attributes and discuss several exemplars with and without these attributes.

Attribute 1: A Shared Passion

If society's members share a passion and commitment to continued prosperity and existence, they will do what it takes to ensure that result. The evidence of this can be seen in twentieth- and twenty-first-century startup nations and companies. Israel is one example amongst modern nations as evidence of the importance and shared passion, commitment, and goals.[1] There are other significant examples in earlier Western history, including the United Provinces that became the Dutch Republic (today, the Netherlands) and the United States. The United Provinces, the young Dutch nation in Europe's north, rebelled against the all-powerful Spanish branch of the Habsburg Empire in the sixteenth century.[2] The Dutch lacked the resources of their Spanish masters, who combined the firepower of its leading military power of the day with the fabulous wealth of the gold bullion mined in South America. They were, nonetheless, defeated by the Dutch upstarts whose commitment to the cause of their independence saw great feats of bravery and ingenuity.

Lacking natural resources forced the Dutch to innovate and engage citizenry in the effort to fight for the young nation's existence. Developing strategies to address external threats was not nearly as important as the ability to pull together the citizenry to fight against those threats. A similar paradigm can be seen in the examples of the American Revolution in its fight against its all-powerful British rulers.

The spirit of a startup is, of course, generally exemplified by technology companies like Google and Facebook. The success of such companies, whose existences were precarious at the start, is due to more than innovation and a great product. Yahoo! Erstwhile CEO Marissa Meyer made a splash when she called for a return to Yahoo!'s roots as a startup recognizing that the vital energy of the startup is a valuable commodity. However, it may not be so easy, indeed Meyer found this out the hard way, to recreate that spirit. When a company is small and growing, each employee feels a strong alignment between his very identity and that of the company. Each employee is preternaturally alert to the threats and risks, which abound on all sides. Most startup companies fail for a number of reasons but mostly because the risks to the company's future from both internal and external forces are greater than at any other stage of the company development cycle. Those companies that do survive and prosper do so in part because of their effectiveness in identifying and addressing the risks to their existence. Though the risks are great, the levels of motivation, if it can be tapped effectively, is even greater. How many search companies were competing with Google? How many social networking companies were competing with Facebook?

The motivation of employees to give back to their community, their company, is most clearly visible in a successful startup. Why do people work the hours they do in a startup? Could it be in part because of a desire for the community and colleagues within that community to do well? Working hard will increase their chances of succeeding. Avoiding risky behavior and errors can be tied back to the same motivation.

"Only the paranoid survive" is the well-known adage originated by Andy Grove of Intel.[3] There is surely something in it. Maintaining a culture of awareness of the risks and threats and the sense that all members of the community need to play their part in countering them is hard to do. But it is probably the one thing that separates out those who survive from those who don't. If a company can tap the passion of its employees to make them paranoid about risks every day, then maybe the startup can survive and prosper. This should not just be how startups operate but how every company operates if it wishes to manage risk effectively.

The question is, how do countries and companies retain that startup passion? How do they hold on to the sense that everyone cares, to the extent, that they are not simply paranoid about their own survival but also about the survival and prosperity of the larger group or country? In the case of the United States, one saw the startup unity give way to division in the Civil War. One can see the same thing happening in the case of Israel. The sense of shared passion and unification of a people against a common threat weakens as the country matures and the immediate perils wax and wane. The startup fails unless it can take things to the next level of maturity—shared values.

Attribute 2: Shared Ethical Values

Adherence to a set of ethical values is the second key attribute for societies wishing to manage risk effectively. Having passion is important, but it needs to be directed toward a common goal and set of objectives. An agreed set of ethical values helps to keep internal threats to a minimum and creates the effective basis for the rule of law.

The nascent Dutch Republic shared a set of religious beliefs based around the Calvinist church.[4] It was really this set of beliefs that differentiated the rebels against their Spanish rulers. The young civil society was founded around two core Calvinist philosophical pillars: first, a work ethic that placed a premium on work and merit as opposed to nobility of birth, and, second, religious tolerance. Agreement to these ground rules was what created the glue to enable a vital and vigorous society to emerge. Internal threats posed by, for example, Hapsburg supporters who could have formed a dangerous alliance with the pro-Hapsburg Belgium were never able to muster sufficient support to pose an internal threat to the revolt.

One can see from the US Civil War how dangerous disagreement on basic core values can be to emerging internal threats. The rift that was formed in the young republic was to no small extent due to ethical and ideological disagreements. Disagreement on the issue of slavery was the focal point, ultimately, in the rift between the North and the South that could only be resolved by a Civil War that cost the lives of hundreds of thousands of Americans. Force was the tool, but the majority shared the view that slavery should end and also that people had equal rights regardless of race and color. Ultimately, the agreement over a set of core values enabled the republic's continued growth and prosperity.[5]

One can see in Israel the impact of ideological splits down religious and ethical lines. The place of the very religious, for instance, and whether they should serve in the Army, and whether or not land should be exchanged for peace have both led to significant rifts in that society. The rift poses a serious risk to the state and highlights the importance of a shared set of beliefs in confronting internal threats. Recalling the Israeli withdrawals from the Sinai Peninsula and from the Gaza Strip, for example, there were scenes of violence with some settlers only leaving after the use of force by Israeli soldiers. There are now over a million very religious Jews who live in Israel. The vast majority of them do not serve in the army or pay taxes.[6] There was once an agreement to subsidize the religious community, that there was a place in a Jewish society for Torah scholars; however, the concept was intended to cover a small number, maybe a few thousand, of truly gifted scholars. As the numbers have increased by the hundreds of thousands, the consensus has broken down and the rift poses a major internal threat to the future of Israel. Another rift has formed between those who wish to give up land for peace and those who do not. The assassination of Prime Minister Rabin by Yigal Amir and the murder of Arabs in Jerusalem by Baruch Goldstein have been the clearest manifestations of this rift. While such actions continue to be opposed by public opinion and law enforcers continue to have the full support of most citizens, one wonders how robust this consensus around democratic and secular values will remain to be and how effective this can continue to be in countering rogue threats.

Germany's post–World War I descent into chaos and the arrival of the Nazis at the helm of German power is a solid example of how rogue threats to the healthy functioning of a state, if not effectively countered, can lead to a state's effective destruction. The Nazi message found fertile ground in a world that was falling apart financially. The feckless and irresponsible policies of the kaiser that led to defeat in World War I[7] were forgotten in favor of a narrative that pinned blame on Jews and Communists who were seen to be exploiting the weakness of the German nation for their own advantage. It took World War II and the destruction of a majority of Jews in Europe for a consensus in favor of a democratic, secular state in Germany.

This lesson should not be lost on banks and other commercial institutions. Just as important for such organizations is agreement on the basic rules of the game, the cultural currency of the environment, and the right of the institution to enforce them. Surprisingly, just as in broader society, one cannot assume that such a consensus exists, but it is equally essential in countering rogue elements. The dynamic at play in a commercial entity, especially a bank or other type of financial institution, is one between the individual and his search for profit and the bank's objectives. The bank relies on the individual to seek a profit but within an agreed framework and within the context of a broad set of rewards. Widespread flouting of trader limits, traders conspiring with controllers, bankers sharing confidential information with colleagues, and so on, all pose potentially existential threats to a bank but cannot take place in the context of strong agreement on the rules and the ethics of the bank. With a group of employees passionate about the firm, agreed values will also ensure their cooperation in identifying potential rogue elements before they can do too much damage.

Successful companies instill a common set of beliefs and values in their employees. If they are strongly instilled, employees tend to do the right thing, however that is defined. Google's "Don't be Evil" is likely the most well-known summary of a firm's values. Other firms, though, such as Disney and Sony, have clear sets of values that employees appear to share. Goldman Sachs and Bridgewater Associates are good examples of explicitly stated values within the financial services sector, and it is hard to think of a rogue trading incident in either case.

Bridgewater Associates is a very successful hedge fund. Its growth to an investment entity with over $80 billion under management has been rapid. Its founder, Ray Dallio, has attracted attention, however, not just as a result of a successful investment strategy, but also a unique management philosophy. *Principles*, a hundred-page text that is required reading for Bridgewater's new hires, sets out the principles that employees are expected to follow to guide them in their work on a daily basis.[8]

Goldman Sachs employees have shown outstanding commitment to uphold certain standards of professional behavior and values. On occasion, this may mean working in the gray areas, but not as rogues but as a company authorized strategy. The success that Goldman enjoyed through deploying effective risk management activities through the 2008 Financial Crisis demonstrated the flexible but broadly defined boundaries that employees work within and the complex structures of decision making. Furthermore, Goldman has not shrunk from firing employees who they have felt overstepped the bounds regardless of how much they made for the firm. Taking such aggressive steps puts employees on notice that there is a set of rules that they must live by or else suffer the consequences.

Attribute 3: Willingness to Debate Issues—The Open Society

When things go wrong and bad and unexpected things happen, there are two possible reactions: either put your head in the sand and pretend it was just bad luck or study what happened, acknowledge your mistakes, and fix them so that it doesn't happen again.

The Chinese and Soviet communist regimes both at different points in time attempted to cover up disasters. These provide useful case studies for the axiom that the cover-up is usually worse than the original incident. Without dynamic, real-time, honest debate and interaction between leaders, managers, and people, incident aftermaths will fester and potentially lead to replays or a failure to correct.

The Chernobyl nuclear disaster occurred on April 26, 1986, and is still widely considered to be the worst nuclear disaster in history. While news of the disaster was being reported in the United States, the playing of music replaced news broadcasts in the Soviet Union. The general population of the Soviet Union was first informed of the disaster only two days after the event. At that time, the reports vastly understated the scale of the damage. The response to contain the damage and get people to safety was slow and unsophisticated. With the general population kept in ignorance, there was no public screaming for help or offering to help. Can you imagine how long it would have taken to identify the Boston Marathon bombers without the ability to enlist the help of the public? Steps were taken by the Soviet government that one can't imagine in an open society. In another example, in an attempt to dilute contaminated meat, the Soviet government mixed small amounts of radiation-tainted cow carcasses with uncontaminated beef before shipping the toxic mix across the country. No less a person than Mikhail Gorbachev has called Chernobyl a "turning point that opened the possibility of a much greater freedom of expression, to the point that the system as we know it could no longer continue." Continuing to conduct such complex and weighty management issues in secret had become untenable.[9]

The SARS epidemic in China provides a second useful case study. The outbreak of severe acute respiratory syndrome (SARS) began in the Guangdong province of China, which borders Hong Kong, in November 2002. Chinese authorities did not report the incident to the World Health Organization (WHO) until February 2003, by which time there were already 305 reported cases and at least five deaths. Contact with outside media and the WHO was discouraged by the Chinese government and a WHO team that had traveled to Beijing was prohibited from visiting the Guangdong Province for a few weeks. Such actions slowed down the possibility of international cooperation to counter and mitigate the threat. This resulted in international criticism, provoking the Chinese Health Minister to apologize for the reporting delays and the Chinese government to issue directives that the press should not refrain from delivering bad news. Unlike the Soviets, the Chinese Communists appear to be able to coexist with a society that can be at times critical of its decisions and crisis management. When China suffered a new strain of avian flu (the H7N9 virus), the government promptly reported on the event and widely shared information pertaining to the outbreak. This response was noticeably different from that following the SARS outbreak. Indeed, the WHO praised China for its actions in quickly reporting and sharing information. Who knows how many lives this may have saved? The moral is clear: Err on the side of sharing too much, rather than too little, information, and ensure that society's leaders are not invested in structures of power whose existence depend on keeping information on "embarrassing" incidents away from the public eye.

As it goes with countries and national systems of leadership and authority, so it goes with firms. An unwillingness to acknowledge internal issues and to share information across the enterprise inevitably leads to a failure to address them properly and a greater risk of reoccurrence. I have discussed the importance of sharing information, for example, about Rogue Traders, trade execution issues, external fraud, and so on up and down and across the organization. Sharing information proactively is only the first step in the process. An open forum for identifying the potential missteps and sources of error in an environment free from recrimination is the important next step. Such a forum can only take place in an organization where the leadership gives its blessing. A lot of attention is paid to fancy analytics and predictive data capabilities. However, first it is important for everyone to understand what just happened, not what may or may not happen in the future.

Bridgewater Associates is a leader in this area in financial service. Founder Ray Dallio has sought to embed the principle of open self-analysis and honest debate about issues and errors. When confusions arise, he has said, it is important to discuss them openly, even if that involves publicly pointing out people's mistakes—a process he referred to as "getting in sync." He added, "I believe that the biggest problem that humanity faces is an ego sensitivity to finding out whether one is right or wrong and identifying what one's strengths and weaknesses are."[10] For senior employees joining Bridgewater as lateral hires, this can seem strange and uncomfortable. The results, however, appear to support the strategy. Bridgewater has been and continues to be a very successful organization.

Attribute 4: Education

An educated citizenry is critical if society is going to be able to manage its risks effectively. We discussed Seligman in Chapter 20 and his theories of happiness. An engaged citizenry is a happy citizenry. Education fuels engagement and opportunities for advancement leading to greater levels of fulfillment. Enhanced ability to manage risks is not the goal of such education, but it is an important byproduct. Education and understanding allied with opportunities for advancement create a citizenry with a strong stake to push back against the status quo, enabling greater focus on those things all around that can threaten to take that away.

The example of fighting terrorism relies on an educated populace for both specifics as well as general information. The population of London was fairly well educated in the dangers of terrorism and previously played a role in identifying potential terrorist threats in everyday life during the 1970s, thanks to IRA bombing campaigns and educational programs that followed in their wake. The 9/11 attacks were visited on a New York and US populace relatively innocent and comparatively uneducated regarding the threat posed by terrorists. Now New York has its eyes wide open for terrorism. The Times Square bomb plot of May 2010 was actually foiled by two street vendors alert to the danger. One wonders if they would have noticed such a threat prior to 9/11. Now, of course, other attacks have been visited in the US on Boston, San Bernardino, Orlando, Minneapolis, and Columbus, other cities relatively innocent to terrorism and so now the education process will kick off more broadly. The lessons from one city should really be transferred to other cities before disasters strike them, too.

A high level of education leads to an educated defense force, police force, and other critical risk management institutions of a self-aware society. The Israel Defense Forces, for example, has no separate officer corps; rather, every citizen joins at the same level, and progress through the ranks is based on time served and merit. This is the risk manager par excellence, its members alive to threats posed continually from within and outside the country, continually in a state of high readiness for action to counter any such active threat.

In translating this lesson to the corporate venue, one finds a lot of parallels. First, one does find that companies that seek out the highest levels of academic excellence in their employees are rewarded by employees with high levels of motivation and behavior that generally conforms to the company codes of ethics and behaviors. Second, if companies actually invest in exciting learning programs for their employees, they can succeed in achieving higher levels of excellence. Training in risk and compliance issues can be important tools for creating employees engaged and aware of these important issues. Lastly, by offering younger employees the opportunity to get involved in senior discussions about risk, as if there is no gulf between senior officers and junior employees, firms can create the type of apprenticeship training model that will likely have more impact than anything strictly classroom-based. Senior leaders can benefit from the lessons from the trenches they learn about from their frontline troops, while their more junior colleagues can benefit from the wisdom and experience of their leaders.

Attribute 5: Interconnectedness

Seligman's third source of happiness comes from the interconnectedness of people. Societies that foster close connections and relationships can monitor what is going on more easily. When children or others get involved in rogue actions, it is generally those who have somehow become unmoored from the normal bonds of society. The society of today places a premium on the number rather than the quality and depth of connections. People count their friends on Facebook, but a large number of virtual friends does not make them any more connected in reality. Yet the breaking of communal bonds is nothing new for American society, which has long encouraged the tearing up of the roots of communities in search of riches and the next frontier. This dynamic has long fostered the development of the isolated and rugged individualist in search of personal freedom. If one looks at the statistics regarding personal mobility, one sees that people are far more likely to move around from place to place in the United States than other Western democracies. This mobility weakens connections within societies and thus makes societies likely more vulnerable to individuals planning rogue and mass murderous actions, both because such people may feel alienated and because fewer people are involved with them to discourage or to monitor what they are doing. The shockingly high number of mass murder events in the United States appears to correlate with a society that has grown increasingly disconnected. Of course, there are other factors involved—prevalence of weapons and inadequate support for the mentally ill—but this factor seems to be underestimated in its influence.

When one looks at primitive tribal societies, there is certainly no shortage of weapons for citizens to use against one another. However, rogue actions are a rarity. Another example of a society with close social bonds and a high incidence of weapons are Israel and the communal life on a kibbutz. Amoz Oz's novel *Elsewhere, Perhaps* is about life on a kibbutz and, among other things, about the positive role of gossip in modifying the antisocial behaviors exhibited by some members of the kibbutz.[11] In such societies as these, abruptly vicious, murderous actions are fewer and far between. In a society with loose social bonds, aberrant and abhorrent behaviors do not come up against the tough judgments and influence of family members, friends, and neighbors and so can go smoothly from harmless fantasy to terrifying reality.

By translating these lessons to the corporate arena, companies that succeed in building strong connections between employees will see better teamwork and less rogue activity. Why damage the people you respect; why take risks that may result in damaging the interests of the team you work with; and, how can you take unauthorized risks if your activities are discussed with superiors and colleagues? Like the kibbutz and the tribe, a firm that is a good risk manager emphasizes the personal and seeks to build connections between employees.

Notes

1. *Start-Up Nation* by Dan Senor and Saul Singer (New York: Hachette Book Group, 2009) addresses the question: How is it that Israel—a country of 7.1 million, only 60 years old, surrounded by enemies, in a constant state of war since its founding, with no natural resources—produces more startup companies than large, peaceful, and stable nations like Japan, China, India, Korea, Canada, and the United Kingdom? The book explores the lessons of the country's adversity-driven culture, which flattens hierarchy and elevates informality.

2. The Dutch revolt in the sixteenth century was seen at the time as a most unlikely David vs. Goliath episode. In many ways, the Dutch republic had many factors in its favor. Geoffrey Parker's *The Dutch Revolt* (Ithaca, NY: Cornell University

Press, 1977), a well-written and concise (less than 300 pages) book remains an excellent introduction to the revolt and the factors behind its success.

3. Only the paranoid survive: As CEO, Andy Grove helped Intel to become the world's largest chip maker and one of the most admired companies in the world. In *Only the Paranoid Survive* (New York: Random House, 1996), Grove discusses how to deal with the moment when massive change occurs and a company must, virtually overnight, adapt or fall by the wayside. Grove calls such a moment a *strategic inflection point,* which can be set off by almost anything: mega-competition, a change in regulations, or a seemingly modest change in technology. When a strategic inflection point hits, the ordinary rules of business go out the window. Yet, managed right, this can be a wonderful growth opportunity.

4. The Spanish Habsburg rulers attempted to impose Catholicism on its Dutch dominion. The prevalence of reformist thinking, including the ideas of John Calvin, were a provocation to the Dutch, who in any case resisted the imposition of absolute rule on their independence. The religious beliefs in opposition to those of their Spanish rulers played a significant role in sustaining the revolt, and the ideas spawned by these philosophies, particularly the religious tolerance fostered by their Protestant beliefs, have underpinned Dutch social and political culture to this day.

5. There is, of course, no shortage of great histories of the American Civil War. The United States today remains a country riven by great ideological differences. There are very few ethical issues that find a consensus amongst the population. Unlike, for instance, the United Kingdom, where there is more or less a consensus against capital punishment and in favor of gun control, there is no such consensus in the United States. Perhaps the only consensus is one in favor of the greatness and exceptionalism of the United States, even if no one can agree on what the exact source of that greatness is.

6. Since Ben Gurion struck a deal with the national Religious Party to exempt a small number of yeshiva students from mandatory military service, the rapid growth in the number of the very religious element of the Jewish population in Israel has created a significant problem for Israeli society. The current estimate is that there are between 1.3 and 1.5 million ultra-orthodox Jews in Israel, as much as 25 percent of the population. This represents a very significant growth in their number and relative political and cultural strength, growth that is only accelerating. Secular Jews are increasingly resentful of the fact that they shoulder the burden in military and financial terms for the religious.

7. Colin Storer, *A Short History of the Weimar Republic* (New York: I.B.Tauris & Co Ltd, 2013), is a useful introduction to post–World War I Germany and the causes of its failure. A. J. P. Taylor has also written widely on the Weimar Republic and the causes of its failure, for instance, see *Origins of the Second World War* (Robbinsdale, MN: Fawcett Books, 1961).

8. John Cassidy, "How Ray Dallio Built the World's Richest and Strangest Hedge Fund," *New Yorker* (July 25, 2011), is an excellent introduction to the philosophy and history of Bridgewater Associates.

9. Mark Joseph Stern, "Did Chernobyl Cause the Soviet Union to Explode? The Nuclear Theory of the Fall of the Soviet Union," *Slate* (January 25, 2013).

10. Cassidy's article in the *New Yorker* is the principal basis for these comments, in addition to friends who have worked at Bridgewater Associates.

11. Amos Oz, *Elsewhere, Perhaps* (New York: Harcourt Brace & Company, 1973).

CHAPTER 25

Conclusion: Seven Traits for Successfully Managing Cognitive Risk

anks have been wrestling with the issues and processes I have been discussing in this book for the past several decades. These days, it is never enough for banks and other financial services companies to merely take risks. Firms must calibrate their risks and monitor them as much as they project return on investment. Every prudent risk is taken with an eye toward avoiding the imprudent one.

It is now a given for any high-functioning, risk-taking institution to have an internal department—or departments—devoted full-time to measuring and setting the firm's risk meter. I call this a company's *risk organization*. Supervised companywide by the chief risk officer, the risk organization comprises managers who report to the CRO, including those tasked with overseeing specific risk areas (operational risk, market risk, credit risk, etc.), as well as business-line managers directly attuned to the risk sensitivity of each revenue center.

Banks that are prioritizing the risk organization are seeing ever-increasing resources devoted to risk management. However, those resources alone do not achieve effective risk management. High-functioning risk organizations I have observed and worked with share and exhibit certain common traits. Here is my list of the seven traits that increase the likelihood of success.

Mature Governance Structure

The first trait of a high-functioning risk organization is a mature risk governance framework. This establishes the objectives, principles, and action plan for how the risk organization will manage risk, as well as the structure of committees and other bodies where key managers discuss risk-related issues and ensure that action items are followed.

Whatever technologies and complex risk management processes a bank has put in place, nothing will work if the organization does not construct an effective risk governance framework. The framework addresses the following questions: How quickly do problems get escalated, and are they escalated to the right people? Are the right people involved in the governance of risk? Are there appropriate working groups and subcommittees to address ongoing issues? When things do go wrong, are the decision makers aware of the root causes, and how are those causes being addressed?

When a company is hurt by a risk failure in some trading unit or branch, it is often a failure of leadership to understand and then question how unusual levels of profit are really being generated by individuals or trades. Think of various rogue-trading failures or the subprime lending debacle. Problem identification may not have occurred, or it may not have been escalated effectively. A risk governance framework can address both of these needs.

Top-to-Bottom Risk Culture

The second trait is a living and breathing risk management culture. A risk governance framework is only helpful if the culture allows those with lower-level responsibilities to take action where they see unusual or unexpected risk exposure. The tone for being proactive is set from the top. An effective CRO spends time on the trading floor and in the branches making sure that everyone in the company receives the message: It is not just risk managers who manage risk, but all employees.

This is an important message because it is those on the front line who ultimately make the difference. Do they know why it is important not to open the door to someone who does not have a proper ID card? Do they understand how opening that phishing email can unlock the company's network? The tone that is set by those at the top can make a vital difference to those who execute on a day-to-day basis. Are senior executives acting in a way that demonstrates and reinforces the importance of the risk message?

An Open Mind about Regulation

Third, effective risk organizations see regulatory requirements not just as a bureaucratic overhead but as an opportunity to strengthen business decision making.

For example, one CRO has discussed with me the applicability of scenario-based stress tests required under the Dodd-Frank Act beyond regulatory compliance. Since the stress test model had to be created anyway, the CRO reasoned, why not also develop it as a tool that can support business case analysis and decision making for a wide range of business purposes?

The same is true for developing an operational risk framework that, while being required by the regulators, can have broader utility. Some banks view it as a check-the-box exercise, but the winners turn it into a data-based risk decision-making tool.

Understanding the Firm's Unique Risk Profile

Fourth, high-functioning risk organizations have a high level of self-awareness of the types of risks that they are prepared to take and the boundaries that they should stay within. We discussed this in relation to Berkshire Hathaway and Facebook earlier in the book. Both these companies have been amply rewarded in the marketplace for their risk management successes in this regard.

On the flip side, the consequences for firms that lack self-awareness and fail to understand the limits of the risks that they take pay a heavy price. The failures of firms such as Knight Capital in market technology, Bear Stearns in managing client assets, and Rochdale Securities in providing customized brokerage services are all such examples.

Not Just Throwing Money at the Problem

The fifth trait is a constant search for efficiency: how to carry out effective risk management with fewer resources. The growth in risk management spending since 2008 is undisputed and potentially unavoidable, given the short-term need to address regulatory requirements, such as those connected to Dodd-Frank, including the Volcker Rule. The winners, however, are those organizations that over the long term can manage their risk and regulatory requirements effectively while on a tighter budget.

Innovation and Technology

The sixth trait is a drive to do research and invest in technology. In the past, this has led to the development of tools such as value-at-risk (VaR) and various risk-scenario tools. Today, organizations that have prioritized innovation can analyze data in more powerful ways to identify emerging risks more quickly and accurately. Those organizations that have outsourced certain repetitive tasks have nurtured a rich risk talent pool to focus on solving difficult analytical questions. They will be able to make the best use of new analytical tools, and will be more sophisticated in managing key risk categories such as anti–money laundering, capital market manipulation, insider trading, and potential global market dislocations. In the future, managing these risks with such tools should become more like managing the traffic of a busy city: Jams will surely occur, but they won't lead to major take-downs.

Constant Self-Analysis

Perhaps the most important trait is a bank's ability and willingness to improve risk management elements that are lacking, which hinder the institution's success. Managing the transformation into a high-functioning risk organization is a long-term but still vital endeavor.

It starts with the ability to look in the mirror and conduct an honest and accurate assessment of the organization in relation to each of these traits and identify where the company falls short. When a company is hit by a high-profile risk failure, it is natural to ask which risk management shortcomings the episode revealed, and then try to address those shortcomings. But an even more winning strategy would be to avoid knee-jerk reactions, asking enough skeptical questions about any efforts to fill gaps—to ensure the new initiative is indeed a right fit for the organization—so the business isn't blinded by its own sense of immediacy.

The acquisition of these seven traits is not simple, but developing the right path will ultimately bring significant rewards to those able to navigate it.

Index

Note: Page references followed by f and t indicate an illustrated figure and table, respectively.